YOUR reci~~pe~~
could appe~~ar~~
in our nex~~t~~
cookbook!

Share your tried & true family favorites with us instantly at
www.gooseberrypatch.com
If you'd rather jot 'em down by hand, just mail this form to...
Gooseberry Patch • Cookbooks – Call for Recipes
PO Box 812 • Columbus, OH 43216-0812

If your recipe is selected for a book, you'll receive a FREE copy!

Please share only your original recipes or those that you have made your own over the years.

Recipe Name:

Number of Servings:

Any fond memories about this recipe? Special touches you like to add
or handy shortcuts?

Ingredients (include specific measurements):

Instructions (continue on back if needed):

Special Code: **cookbookspage**

Over ➤

Extra space for recipe if needed:

Tell us about yourself...

Your complete contact information is needed so that we can send you your FREE cookbook, if your recipe is published. Phone numbers and email addresses are kept private and will only be used if we have questions about your recipe.

Name:

Address:

City: State: Zip:

Email:

Daytime Phone:

Thank you! Vickie & Jo Ann

Grandma's Best
COMFORT FOODS

Handed-down favorite recipes from
the comfort of Grandma's kitchen.

Gooseberry Patch

An imprint of Globe Pequot
246 Goose Lane
Guilford, CT 06437

www.gooseberrypatch.com

1•800•854•6673

Copyright 2022, Gooseberry Patch 978-1-62093-444-9

Do you have a tried & true recipe...

tip, craft or memory that you'd like to see featured in
a **Gooseberry Patch** cookbook? Visit our website at
www.gooseberrypatch.com and follow the
easy steps to submit your favorite family recipe.
Or send them to us at:

Gooseberry Patch
PO Box 812
Columbus, OH 43216-0812

Don't forget to include the number of servings your recipe makes,
plus your name, address, phone number and email address. If we
select your recipe, your name will appear right along with it...
and you'll receive a **FREE** copy of the book!

Contents

Dedication

To families everywhere who have made wonderful memories together over delicious dishes.

Appreciation

Thanks to all of you who generously shared your favorite recipes from Grandma.

RISE & SHINE,
It's Breakfast Time

Grandma's Best COMFORT FOODS

Gladys's Brunch Coffee Cake

Page Lindstrom
Ellsworth, WI

This is a delicious treat for breakfast or dessert! It is my husband's grandma's recipe...she used to make it for him all the time. She has passed, so now I make it for him.

8-oz. pkg. cream cheese, softened
1/2 c. butter
1-1/4 c. sugar
2 eggs, beaten
1 t. vanilla extract

2 c. all-purpose flour
1 t. baking powder
1/2 t. baking soda
1/4 t. salt
1/3 c. milk

In a large bowl, beat cream cheese, butter and sugar until light and fluffy. Add eggs and vanilla; beat well and set aside. In a separate bowl, mix flour, baking powder, baking soda and salt. Add flour mixture to butter mixture alternately with milk, beating until smooth. Spread batter in a greased and floured 13"x9" baking pan. Spread Topping over all. Bake at 350 degrees for 30 to 35 minutes. Cut into squares. Makes 16 servings.

Topping:

1/2 c. brown sugar, packed
1/2 c. all-purpose flour

3 T. butter
1 t. cinnamon

Mix together all ingredients until crumbly.

Stir a spoonful of strawberry jam or orange marmalade
into a cup of hot tea for extra sweetness.

RISE & SHINE,
It's Breakfast Time

Breakfast Soufflé

Panda Spurgin
Bella Vista, AR

This delicious breakfast recipe was always a family favorite when we gathered during the holidays. It's an easy overnight make-ahead dish.

9 eggs, beaten
3 c. milk
1-1/2 t. dry mustard
1 t. salt
3 slices white bread, cubed

1-1/2 c. shredded Cheddar cheese
1-1/2 lbs. favorite ground pork sausage, browned and drained

In a large bowl, whisk together eggs, milk and seasonings. Fold in bread, cheese and browned sausage. Transfer mixture to a greased 3-quart casserole dish; cover and refrigerate overnight. Uncover and bake at 350 degrees for one hour, or until heated through. Serves 8.

Toad in a Hole, Egg in a Nest...whatever the name, kids love 'em and they're so easy to fix. Cut out the center of a slice of bread with a small cookie cutter. Add the bread to a buttered skillet over medium heat and break an egg into the hole. Cook until golden on the bottom, turn over with a spatula and cook until the egg is set as you like.

Peanutty Breakfast Ring

Alice Joy Randall
Nacogdoches, TX

My husband and I really like this recipe. It was originally called a tea ring, but we enjoy it for breakfast. It came from a home economics teachers' recipe book that I purchased from a neighbor, over 40 years ago. It is so easy, yet so delicious.

1/4 c. butter, melted
1 c. peanuts, finely chopped
7-1/2 oz. tube refrigerated
    plain or buttermilk biscuits,
    separated

1/2 c. powdered sugar
1 T. water
Garnish: soft butter spread

Place butter in a small bowl; place peanuts in another small bowl. Dip both sides of biscuits in melted butter and then into peanuts, coating well. Arrange biscuits in an overlapping circle on a greased baking sheet. Bake at 425 degrees for 10 to 15 minutes, until golden. In a separate small bowl, mix powdered sugar and water; drizzle at once over hot biscuits. Slide onto a serving plate and serve warm with a soft butter spread. Serves 4.

A single vintage quilt patch makes a cozy topper for
a bread basket...just stitch it to a large napkin in
a matching color.

RISE & SHINE,
It's Breakfast Time

Earleen's Western-Style Oven Omelet

*Pat Beach
Fisherville, KY*

My sister took a recipe she had for an oven omelet and made a few additions to it. We made it for our husbands when they came back from early morning fishing, and they raved about it with each bite! They both agreed that it tastes like a western omelet.

8 eggs
1 c. milk
2 c. frozen diced hashbrowns, thawed
4-oz. can sliced mushrooms, drained
1 c. cooked ham, diced

1 c. shredded Cheddar cheese
1/2 c. green pepper, finely chopped
1/4 c. onion, finely chopped
3/4 to 1 t. salt
pepper to taste

Beat eggs in a large bowl; whisk in milk. Stir in remaining ingredients; transfer to a lightly greased 9"x9" baking pan. Bake, uncovered, at 350 degrees for 45 to 50 minutes, or 55 to 60 minutes for a deep pan, until a knife tip inserted in the center comes out clean. Makes 6 servings.

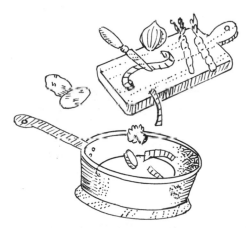

Omelets and scrambles are perfect for using up all kinds of odds & ends from the fridge. Mushrooms, tomatoes and asparagus are especially good with eggs. Slice or dice veggies and sauté until tender...scrumptious! Grandma would approve of your thriftiness.

Hashbrown Potato Quiche

Linda Davidson
Lexington, KY

This is a tasty breakfast served with buttered toast and jelly.
It is great to take to a dinner at church, too!

3 c. frozen shredded hashbrown
   potatoes, thawed
1/3 c. butter, melted
1 c. cooked ham, chopped
1 c. shredded Cheddar cheese
1/4 c. green or red pepper,
   chopped

1/4 c. onion, chopped
2 eggs, beaten
1/2 c. milk
1/2 t. salt
1/4 t. pepper

Spread potatoes out on paper towels to remove some of the moisture.
Pat potatoes into the bottom and up the sides of an ungreased 9" pie
plate. Drizzle with butter, making sure to cover the edges. Bake,
uncovered, at 425 degrees for 25 minutes; reduce oven to 350 degrees.
Layer ham, cheese, green or red pepper and onion over baked crust.
In a bowl, whisk together remaining ingredients; pour over all. Bake,
uncovered, at 350 degrees for 25 minutes, or until a knife tip inserted in
the center comes out clean. Cut into wedges to serve. Makes 8 servings.

Come along inside...we'll see if tea and buns
can make the world a better place.
–Kenneth Grahame

RISE & SHINE,
It's Breakfast Time

Dippy Eggs & Toast Soldiers

Regina Vining
Warwick, RI

My Great-Gram Margaret came from England. Whenever we kids spent the weekend at her house, she would make this special breakfast for us, remembered from her own childhood. She had the sweetest little vintage egg cups. We loved dipping the fingers of buttered toast (which she called "soldiers") into the soft-boiled eggs.

2 whole eggs
3 slices favorite bread

softened butter to taste
salt and pepper to taste

Bring a saucepan of water to a boil over medium-high heat. Carefully add unbroken eggs to the water; boil for 5 minutes. Meanwhile, toast bread; trim crusts, if desired. Spread bread with butter; cut bread into one-inch strips. When eggs are done, use a slotted spoon to place each egg in an egg cup. Tap around the top of each egg with a table knife; lift off shell on top. Season eggs with salt and pepper. Serve toast "soldiers" alongside eggs. Serves 2.

It's easy to tell if the eggs in your refrigerator are fresh.
Just place them in a bowl of water...a fresh egg will sink,
but a not-so-fresh egg will float.

Grandma's Best
COMFORT FOODS

Nana's Waffles

Elisha Nelson
Brookline, MO

There's nothing like waking up on Nana's farm and smelling these waffles baking in the kitchen! They're crisp on the outside and fluffy on the inside. Any extra waffles can be wrapped and put in the freezer for up to two months, then reheated in the oven.

1 c. all-purpose flour
1 c. whole-wheat flour
1/4 c. oat flour (or additional
    whole-wheat flour)
1-1/2 T. sugar
4 t. baking powder
3/4 t. salt

2 eggs, beaten
2-1/4 c. milk
1/2 c. butter, melted
Optional: chopped pecans, diced
    apples, blueberries
Garnish: butter, maple syrup

In a bowl, mix flours, sugar, baking powder and salt; set aside. In a large bowl, whisk together eggs, milk and butter. Add flour mixture to egg mixture; stir just until blended. Fold in optional ingredients, if desired. Set aside batter to stand for 15 minutes or while the waffle iron preheats. Add batter to the waffle iron by 1/2 cupfuls; cook according to manufacturer's directions. Serve topped with butter and maple syrup. Makes 4 to 6 waffles.

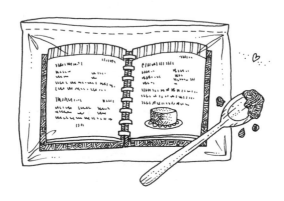

Keep a cherished handed-down cookbook clean and free of spatters. Slip it into a gallon-size plastic zipping bag before cooking up a favorite recipe.

RISE & SHINE,
It's Breakfast Time

New Orleans Banana Flapjacks

Joyceann Dreibelbis
Wooster, OH

Add special charm to your weekend with these Southern-style pancakes...sure to quickly become a breakfast favorite!

2 t. baking soda
2 c. buttermilk
2 c. all-purpose flour
2 eggs, beaten

3 T. butter, melted
2 c. ripe bananas, sliced
Garnish: maple syrup

In a large bowl, dissolve baking soda in buttermilk. Add flour, eggs and butter; stir lightly. Batter should be streaky and lumpy. Gently fold in bananas. Drop by large spoonfuls onto a hot, lightly greased griddle; turn when bubbles begin to break. Cook until golden. Serve with maple syrup. Serves 4 to 6.

Serve waffles, pancakes or biscuits topped with scrumptious maple butter. Simply whip 1/2 cup butter with one cup of maple syrup.

Grandma's Best
COMFORT FOODS

Christopher's Breakfast Muffins

Kathy Neuppert Swanson
Hemet, CA

These yummy muffins make a wonderful breakfast and are a favorite of my nephew, Christopher. I once had them ready for him to enjoy when he was home on leave from the Navy. They melt in your mouth and are extra good because of the bacon...delicious made with 2 cups chopped ham instead of the bacon, too. These muffins are even easy to eat on the run. Oh, yum!

1 lb. bacon
1/2 c. onion, chopped
2 c. self-rising flour

1 c. milk
1 c. mayonnaise
1 c. shredded Cheddar cheese

In a large skillet, cook bacon over medium heat until crisp. Remove bacon with a slotted spoon to drain on paper towels. Add onion to drippings in skillet; cook until softened, about 3 minutes. Remove onion to paper towels. In a large bowl, mix remaining ingredients together until just combined. Stir in crumbled bacon and onion, being careful not to overmix. Spoon batter into 12 greased muffin cups, filling 2/3 full. Bake at 350 degrees for about 15 minutes. Remove muffins to a wire rack as soon as they are cool enough to handle. Makes one dozen.

Use an old-fashioned ice cream scoop to fill muffin cups with batter...no drips, no spills and muffins turn out perfectly sized.

RISE & SHINE,
It's Breakfast Time

Hearty Breakfast Casserole

Dana Brendza
Twinsburg, OH

I like to prepare this casserole ahead of time, keeping the eggs and milk separate until baking, for family weekends at Nana & Papa's lake house. It's a crowd favorite for all ages!

8-oz. tube refrigerated
    crescent rolls
16-oz. pkg. ground pork sage
    breakfast sausage, browned
    and drained
2 c. frozen diced hashbrowns,
    thawed

8-oz. pkg. shredded Cheddar or
    Mexican-blend cheese
onion powder, salt and pepper
    to taste
6 eggs, beaten
1/2 c. whole milk

Press crescent rolls into the bottom of a lightly greased 13"x9" baking pan, sealing edges to form a crust. Top crust with browned sausage, hashbrowns, cheese and seasonings; set aside. Whisk together eggs and milk; pour evenly over top. Bake, uncovered, at 375 degrees for 30 to 40 minutes, until cheese is bubbly and edges are golden. Cut into squares. Serves 8 to 12.

Serve up some sweet memories. Bring out Grandma's vintage toast rack and jelly dish to use on the breakfast table.

Grandma's Best
COMFORT FOODS

Mini Poppy Seed Muffins

Gail Blain
Grand Island, NE

*Muffins are our traditional Sunday morning breakfast. With some
fruit and a pot of hot tea, these lemony minis are perfect as
we get ready for church.*

1-1/3 c. all-purpose flour
1/2 t. baking powder
1/4 t. baking soda
1/8 t. salt
2 T. poppy seed
2/3 c. butter, softened

3/4 c. sugar
2 eggs
1 t. vanilla extract
1/4 t. lemon extract
1/3 c. lemon yogurt

In a bowl, combine flour, baking powder, baking soda, salt and poppy
seed; set aside. In a separate large bowl, combine butter and sugar. Beat
with an electric mixer on medium speed, scraping bowl often, until
creamy. Add eggs, one at a time, beating well after each addition. Add
extracts; mix well. Reduce mixer speed to low. Alternately add flour
mixture and yogurt, beating after each addition, just until moistened.
Spoon batter into paper-lined mini muffin cups, filling 2/3 full. Bake at
350 degrees for 15 to 18 minutes, until set and very lightly golden. Cool
muffins on a wire rack. Makes 3 dozen.

For the tenderest muffins and quick breads, mix batter
just until moistened...a few lumps won't matter!

RISE & SHINE,
It's Breakfast Time

Eggs & Ham Casserole

Edward Kielar
Whitehouse, OH

Your family will love this unusual dish for breakfast on a chilly morning. Save time by assembling the night before, then adding toppings and baking in the morning.

6 eggs, hard-boiled, peeled
   and halved
1/4 c. celery, finely chopped
1 T. mayonnaise
1 t. mustard
6 thin slices deli baked ham

10-3/4 oz. can cream of
   mushroom soup
1/3 c. milk
1/4 c. potato chips, crushed
1/2 c. shredded Cheddar cheese

Remove egg yolks to a small bowl; set aside egg whites. Mash egg yolks with a fork. Add celery, mayonnaise and mustard; mix well. Spoon egg yolk mixture into egg whites; gently press filled egg whites together in pairs. Wrap each filled egg with a ham slice; place seam-side down in a buttered 9"x9" baking pan. In a small bowl, whisk together soup and milk; spoon over eggs. Top with chips and cheese. Bake, uncovered, at 350 degrees for 30 minutes, until hot and bubbly. Serves 6.

Serve up an old-fashioned fruit salad at breakfast...it's easy. Toss together ripe summer fruits like blueberries, strawberries, orange and kiwi slices. Drizzle with a dressing made by whisking together 1/2 cup honey, 1/4 cup lime juice and one teaspoon lime zest.

Grandma's Best
COMFORT FOODS

Grandma's Best
Cinnamon-Sugar Bread

Kim Bugaj
Manchester, CT

*This is an amazing cinnamon bread! The recipe was handed down
from my grandma to my mom, and then Mom handed it down
to me. It tastes so good warm!*

1 T. butter, softened	3/4 t. salt
1-1/3 c. sugar, divided	1 egg, beaten
4 t. cinnamon, divided	1 c. milk
2 c. all-purpose flour	1/3 c. canola oil
1 T. baking powder	1 t. vanilla extract

Coat a 9"x5" loaf pan with butter; set aside. In a small bowl, stir
together 1/3 cup sugar and 3 teaspoons cinnamon; set aside. In a large
bowl, sift together flour, baking powder, salt, remaining cinnamon and
remaining sugar. In another bowl, whisk together egg, milk, oil and
vanilla. Add egg mixture to flour mixture; stir just until combined. Pour
half of batter into loaf pan; sprinkle with half of cinnamon-sugar. Add
remaining batter; use a knife to swirl batter. Top with remaining
cinnamon-sugar. Bake at 350 degrees for 45 minutes, or until a
toothpick inserted in the center comes out clean. Cool in pan on a wire
rack for 10 minutes. Remove loaf from pan onto a plate or small platter.
Carefully press all the sides of the loaf into any cinnamon-sugar that
comes off onto the plate. Slice and serve. Makes one loaf.

A grandma is warm hugs and sweet memories.
She is an encouraging word and a tender touch.
She is full of proud smiles.
–Barbara Cage

RISE & SHINE, *It's Breakfast Time*

Deluxe Apple Oatmeal

Shari Schiltz
New Ulm, MN

This will warm you up on a cold winter morning...yummy!
Add some chopped walnuts or raisins, if you like.

1-3/4 c. water
1 c. quick-cooking oats,
   uncooked
1/8 t. salt
1 apple, cored and diced

1 to 2 T. brown sugar, packed
1/4 c. half-and-half
2 T. cinnamon
2 t. butter

In a saucepan, bring water to a boil over medium heat. Stir in oats and salt; cook over medium heat for one minute. Stir in remaining ingredients and serve. Makes 2 servings.

Blueberry Pancakes

Karen Wilson
Defiance, OH

These are my grandkids' favorite pancakes. They are so light,
sometimes the kids eat them plain, with no butter or syrup!

2 eggs, separated
1 c. all-purpose flour
2 T. sugar
1 t. baking powder
1/8 t. baking soda

1 t. salt
1 c. buttermilk
2 T. butter, melted
1 t. vanilla extract
1 to 1-1/2 c. blueberries

Place egg whites in a small bowl; set aside egg yolks. With an electric mixer on high speed, beat egg whites until stiff peaks form; set aside. In another bowl, combine flour, sugar, baking powder, baking soda and salt; mix well. Stir in egg yolks, buttermilk, melted butter and vanilla; gently fold in beaten egg whites. Fold in blueberries. Let batter stand for 20 minutes. Ladle batter onto a heated, buttered griddle by 1/4 to 1/2 cupfuls. Cook until bubbles appear around the edges; flip pancakes and cook until done on the other side. Makes 12 pancakes.

It's easy to make a jar of crystallized honey useable again. Set it in a small saucepan of simmering water...the crystals will dissolve after several minutes.

19

Charleston Breakfast Bake

Karen Antonides
Gahanna, OH

This is a wonderful make-ahead breakfast bake that our family enjoys, especially during the holidays. My son-in-law loves breakfast and is especially fond of this dish, made with either ham or bacon. It's great if there are leftovers served the next day.

5-oz. pkg. buttery garlic or
    plain croutons
1/4 c. butter, melted
8-oz. pkg. shredded sharp
    Cheddar cheese
9 eggs, beaten
2 c. milk

1 green pepper, diced
2 T. mustard
salt and pepper to taste
12 slices bacon, crisply cooked
    and crumbled, or 2 c. cooked
    ham, diced

Spray a 13"x9" baking pan with non-stick vegetable spray. Spread croutons evenly in pan; drizzle with melted butter. Sprinkle cheese evenly over croutons; set aside. In a large bowl, whisk together remaining ingredients except bacon or ham; pour over cheese. Sprinkle with bacon or ham. Cover with aluminum foil and refrigerate overnight. In the morning, let stand at room temperature 30 minutes before baking. Bake, covered, at 350 degrees for 30 minutes. Remove foil. Bake an additional 30 minutes, or until a knife tip inserted in the center comes out clean. Let stand 10 minutes; cut into squares. Makes 10 to 12 servings.

Invite friends over for a cozy breakfast served on the porch. Make it picture-perfect with a yard or two of striped cotton ticking on the table and a milk bottle filled with just-picked posies...it's super simple.

RISE & SHINE,
It's Breakfast Time

Celebration Grits

Lynnette Jones
East Flat Rock, NC

We host my husband's extended family for a July 4th breakfast. This has been a celebration in his family for over seventy years! Breakfast is cooked outdoors on what we call an outdoor furnace or brick stove, with a few dishes cooked indoors. These grits have become a hit with everyone who loves grits.

2-2/3 c. water	1 c. stone-ground grits,
1-1/2 t. salt	uncooked
1-1/2 c. whipping cream	3 T. butter

Mix all ingredients in a saucepan. Bring to a boil over medium heat. Reduce heat to low and cook for 30 minutes, or longer for a creamier consistency, stirring often while cooking. If too thick, add a little more water or cream to desired consistency. Makes 6 to 8 servings.

When frying bacon for breakfast, tuck a few slices in the refrigerator. Later, slice a homegrown tomato into thick slices and add crisp lettuce and country-style bread for a fresh BLT sandwich...lunch is served!

Grandma's Best COMFORT FOODS

Poppie's French Toast

*Sarah Slaven
Strunk, KY*

When I was growing up, I remember my dad making this French toast. My kids call my dad Poppie...they love it as much as I did and still do, to this day.

5 eggs, beaten
1 T. cinnamon
1/4 c. sugar

8 slices bread
Garnish: maple syrup

Beat eggs in a shallow dish; set aside. Mix cinnamon and sugar together in a cup; sprinkle one tablespoon of mixture into eggs. Dip bread slices into egg mixture; flip to coat both sides. Add bread slices, a few at a time, to a greased skillet over medium heat; sprinkle with more cinnamon-sugar. Cook until golden on both sides. Serve with maple syrup. Makes 4 servings.

Oven-Roasted Redskin Potatoes

*Roberta Simpkins
Mentor on the Lake, OH*

My mom used to make these savory potatoes for dinner. I make them to serve with breakfast or dinner...they reheat very well!

8 redskin potatoes, cubed
1 medium onion, quartered and
   separated into crescents

1/3 c. olive oil
1.35-oz. pkg. onion soup mix

Combine all ingredients in a gallon-size plastic zipping bag. Seal bag; shake several times to coat. Transfer to a 13"x9" baking pan coated with non-stick vegetable spray. Bake, uncovered, at 425 degrees, for about 40 minutes, stirring every 10 minutes, until potatoes are tender and golden. Makes 4 servings.

Set aside day-old bread for making French toast...it absorbs milk better than bakery-fresh bread.

4-Cup Salad

Barbara Treat
Ennis, TX

This is a very quick & easy fruit salad. We all enjoyed it,
and still do. Thank you, Grandma!

1 c. crushed pineapple, drained
1 c. mandarin oranges, drained
1 c. cottage cheese

1 c. frozen whipped topping,
  thawed

Combine all ingredients in a bowl; mix gently. Cover and chill. Makes
4 to 6 servings.

Shirred Eggs

Cathy Hillier
Salt Lake City, UT

An old-fashioned breakfast dish that's simple to make.
Add a basket of warm muffins for a comforting meal.

1/4 t. butter, softened
2 t. whipping cream
2 eggs

1 t. grated Parmesan cheese
1 t. fresh chives, minced
salt and pepper to taste

Coat a 6-ounce ramekin with butter; add cream to ramekin. Crack eggs
into ramekin without breaking yolks. Using a teaspoon, gently move
yolks into the center of the ramekin. Sprinkle eggs with remaining
ingredients. Bake, uncovered, at 325 degrees for 12 to 15 minutes,
until egg whites have set and yolks are still soft. Remove from oven;
let stand 2 to 3 minutes before serving. Serves one.

Extra waffles and pancakes can be frozen separately in plastic
freezer bags for up to a month. Reheat them in a toaster
for a quick breakfast.

Gramma's Apple Biscuit Coffee Cake

Barbara Cebula
Chicopee, MA

This is a recipe handed down from my mother to me. It is very tasty with a cup of hot tea or coffee on a chilly day.

2 T. butter, melted
2 cooking apples, peeled
   and sliced
1/4 c. raisins
8-oz. tube refrigerated biscuits,
   quartered

1/4 c. brown sugar, packed
1/4 c. light corn syrup
1 egg, beaten
1/2 t. cinnamon
Optional: 1/4 c. chopped walnuts
1 T. chilled butter, diced

Spread melted butter in the bottom of a 9" round cake pan. Arrange sliced apples over butter; sprinkle raisins over apples. Arrange biscuit pieces over apples. In a bowl, mix together brown sugar, corn syrup, egg and cinnamon until well blended and brown sugar is dissolved; spoon over biscuits. Sprinkle walnuts over top, if using; dot with chilled butter. Bake at 350 degrees for 25 to 30 minutes. Invert onto a serving place; spoon sugary juices from pan over top. Cut into wedges and serve. Makes 6 to 8 servings.

Serve up a little whimsy with breakfast! Pour pancake batter into squirt bottles and squeeze the batter directly onto a hot, greased griddle to form bunnies, cats or your child's favorite animal.

RISE & SHINE, *It's Breakfast Time*

Old-Fashioned Corned Beef Hash

Marcia Shaffer
Conneaut Lake, PA

Just like Grandma would serve up on a cold winter day.
Serve over grits, biscuits or toast.

2 to 3 t. oil
2 slices bacon, chopped
1 c. onion, chopped
3 potatoes, cubed
12-oz. can corned beef, drained
   and chopped

14-1/2 oz. can diced tomatoes,
   drained
1 t. sugar
1 bay leaf
salt and pepper to taste

Heat oil in a skillet over medium heat; add bacon and onion. Cook until bacon is crisp and onion is caramelized, stirring occasionally. Add potatoes; cook until tender and golden, stirring often. Stir in remaining ingredients. Simmer over low heat for 10 minutes, or until blended well. Discard bay leaf before serving. Makes 4 servings.

Top corned beef hash with a perfectly round fried egg...so pretty on a breakfast plate! Remove both ends of a clean, empty tuna can. To use, set can in a greased skillet, break an egg into it and cook to desired doneness.

Grandma's Best COMFORT FOODS

French Toast with Praline Sauce

Vickie Wiseman
Liberty Township, OH

I can remember making this delicious recipe with my great-grandmother. She taught me that whenever I am using cinnamon, I should add some nutmeg and cardamom to enhance the flavor. I believe this was actually her mother's recipe, from the late 1800s. Grandma always used fresh-baked bread, but any good bread will work.

1 loaf bread, sliced 1-inch thick	2 t. vanilla extract
6 eggs	1 t. cinnamon
1/2 c. whipping cream	1/2 t. nutmeg
1 T. brown sugar, packed	1/4 t. cardamom

Set out bread slices for one to 2 hours to dry. In a large bowl, combine remaining ingredients. Beat with an electric mixer on medium speed until smooth and brown sugar is dissolved. Pour one cup of mixture into a greased 13"x9" baking pan. Arrange bread slices on top; pour remaining egg mixture evenly over bread. Cover and refrigerate overnight. If desired, heat a greased cast-iron skillet or electric griddle. Add bread slices, a few at a time; cook until golden on both sides. (This step adds color to the toast but may be omitted.) Return bread slices to baking pan. Spoon Pecan Praline Syrup over top. Bake at 350 degrees until set and golden, about 30 minutes. Makes 12 servings.

Pecan Praline Syrup:

1 T. butter	1/2 c. pure maple syrup
3/4 c. brown sugar, packed	3/4 c. chopped pecans, toasted

Melt butter in a saucepan over medium heat. Add brown sugar and maple syrup; cook and stir until smooth. Bring mixture to a boil. Reduce heat to low and simmer for one minute, stirring constantly. Stir pecans into syrup.

RISE & SHINE,
It's Breakfast Time

Grandma's Chocolate Gravy

Janice Curtis
Yucaipa, CA

This was made by my grandmother, then my mother and now on to all the grandkids and great-grandkids who love to eat it. Definitely comfort food! It's something like a rich chocolate pudding. Serve it spooned over hot biscuits for breakfast.

1-1/2 c. sugar
3 T. baking cocoa
2 1/2 T. cornstarch

1/8 t. salt
3 c. milk
1 t. vanilla extract

Combine all ingredients in a saucepan; mix well. Cook and stir over medium heat for 7 to 10 minutes, stirring often, until mixture thickens. Makes 4 to 6 servings.

Freezer Strawberry Jam

Pam Hooley
LaGrange, IN

This was Grandma's recipe, and she thought it was the greatest thing since sliced bread when she started making it... she didn't have to can it!

3-1/2 c. ripe strawberries, hulled, sliced and crushed
6-1/2 c. sugar
1 c. water

1-3/4 oz. pkg. powdered fruit pectin
5 to 6 1/2-pt. plastic freezer jars with lids, sterilized

In a large stockpot, mix berries and sugar; cover and let stand for several hours. Add water and pectin; stir well. Bring to a full boil over medium-high heat; boil hard for one minute. Ladle into jars, leaving 1/2-inch headspace. Cool; add lids and store in freezer. To use, thaw overnight in refrigerator. Makes about 5 to 6 cups.

Keep a vintage–style shaker filled with powdered sugar on the breakfast table...handy for sprinkling on pancakes, waffles and French toast.

Grana's Ranch Biscuits

Marty Findley
Boyd, TX

My mother-in-law always made these when we stayed at the family ranch. Originally known as angel biscuits, the grandkids dubbed them Grana's Ranch Biscuits. They were an expected part of breakfast every morning and for every family dinner as well.

1 env. active dry yeast
2 T. very warm water, about
    110 to 115 degrees
2 c. buttermilk
5 c. all-purpose flour, divided
1/4 c. sugar

1 T. baking powder
1 t. baking soda
1-1/4 t. salt
1 c. shortening
Optional: melted butter

In a small bowl, dissolve yeast in warm water; add buttermilk and set aside. In a large bowl, sift together 4 cups flour, sugar, baking powder, baking soda and salt. Cut shortening into flour mixture and mix well. Add yeast mixture and blend well. Spread remaining flour on a work surface. Turn out dough and knead until smooth. (At this stage, dough may be covered and refrigerated, to use as needed.) Roll out dough 1/4-inch thick; cut with a small biscuit cutter or a small juice can. If desired, dip biscuits into melted butter and fold over. Arrange on ungreased baking sheets. Bake at 400 degrees for 15 minutes, or until golden. Makes 5 dozen small biscuits.

For the fluffiest scrambled eggs ever, try Grandma's secret...
stir in a pinch of baking powder.

RISE & SHINE,
It's Breakfast Time

Cheesy Hashbrown Nuggets

Vickie
Gooseberry Patch

*Yum! These are always welcome on a brunch or appetizer buffet.
Swap in your favorite cheese, if you like.*

6 slices bacon
1 egg, beaten
1/2 c. sour cream
salt and pepper to taste

1-1/2 c. shredded sharp
  Cheddar cheese
20-oz. pkg. frozen shredded
  hashbrowns, thawed

Cook bacon in a skillet over medium heat until crisp. Drain; set aside
bacon on paper towels. In a bowl, whisk together egg, sour cream and
seasonings; stir in cheese. Fold in hashbrowns and bacon. Scoop a
heaping tablespoon of hashbrown mixture and make a ball. Add
mixture to well-greased mini muffin cups by heaping tablespoonfuls.
Bake at 425 degrees for 20 minutes, or until hot and golden. Serve
warm. Makes about 2 dozen.

Bacon Roll-Ups

Irene Robinson
Cincinnati, OH

*Easy to make, quick to disappear! Serve these little morsels
with brunch or as a party appetizer.*

1/2 lb. hot ground pork sausage
8-oz. pkg. cream cheese,
  softened

10 slices white bread, crusts
  removed
10 slices bacon, quartered

Brown sausage in a skillet over medium heat; drain. Stir in cream
cheese and set aside. Cut each bread slice into 4 fingers. Spread each
bread strip with a little of sausage mixture; place bread strip on top of a
bacon piece. Roll up jelly-roll fashion; secure with a toothpick. Arrange
roll-ups on an ungreased baking sheet. Bake at 400 degrees for 15 to
20 minutes, until crisp and golden. Makes about 3-1/2 dozen.

Grandma's Best

COMFORT FOODS

Grandma's Breakfast Omelet

Joanne Mauseth
Clear Lake, DE

I just love this for breakfast on Sunday mornings after church! When my parents were first married, my dad asked for an omelet for breakfast. So Mom made him an omelet, but he said, "Not that kind, I want the kind my Mom makes." Grandma told her the recipe, which had never been written down...it was a "little of this & a little of that" kind of thing. Over the years, Mom perfected the recipe, and growing up, it was my favorite breakfast. Still, nothing was written down! After I was married and my daughter was born, I sat down with Mom and we finally wrote down a recipe to hand down to my daughter. I'm happy to share it with you too.

2 eggs, beaten well
1 c. milk
1/4 c. sugar
3/4 to 1 c. all-purpose flour

1 to 2 T. bacon drippings
   or butter
Garnish: butter, pancake syrup

In a bowl, mix eggs, milk and sugar. Stir in enough flour to make a thickened yet pourable batter, the consistency of waffle batter. Melt bacon drippings or shortening in a skillet over medium heat. Pour in enough batter to fill the bottom of skillet, about 1/4-inch. Cook until golden; flip to other side and cook until golden. Cut into bite-size pieces; serve with butter and syrup. Serves 2.

Grandma's kitchen step stool was always so handy for little ones to perch on. Freshen it up now with a new coat of paint and clippings from seed packets découpaged on.

RISE & SHINE,
It's Breakfast Time

Mom-Mom's Buttermilk Breakfast Cake

*Shawna Weida
Emmaus, PA*

*This recipe was passed down from my great-grandmother,
maybe even further back! I remember her baking in her
kitchen. It's easy to make.*

3 c. all-purpose flour
1/2 c. butter, or 1/4 c. butter and
   1/4 c. shortening
2 c. sugar

2 eggs
1 c. buttermilk
1 t. baking soda

In a large bowl, combine flour and butter (or butter and shortening).
Mix thoroughly. Add sugar and mix well until crumbly. Set aside
1/2 cup crumb mixture for topping. In a separate bowl, beat eggs well;
add to flour mixture and stir well. Combine buttermilk and baking soda
in a cup; add to batter, stirring well. If batter is too thick to stir easily,
stir in a little milk. Divide batter between 2 greased and floured 9" round
cake pans; top each with half of reserved crumb mixture. Bake at
350 degrees for 30 to 35 minutes. Makes 2 cakes; each makes 6 to
8 servings.

Tempt fussy kids with grilled cheese sandwiches for breakfast.
Grilled peanut butter sammies are tasty too. Toast sandwiches
on a waffle iron instead of a griddle...kids will love 'em!

Dutch Baby with Spiced Fruit

Staci Prickett
Montezuma, GA

This is an amazing recipe...everyone loves to watch it bake! It puffs up in the oven, then slightly falls when you take it out. I often make this as a late-night treat when I want something a little sweet.

3 T. butter
1/2 c. all-purpose flour
1 T. sugar
1/4 t. salt
1/8 t. nutmeg

1/2 c. milk, room temperature
2 eggs, room temperature, beaten
1 t. vanilla extract
1/8 t. lemon extract
Garnish: powdered sugar

Add butter to a cast-iron skillet; place in oven at 425 degrees to melt. In a bowl, whisk together flour, sugar, salt and spice. Stir in milk, eggs and extracts; whisk until smooth. Remove hot skillet from oven; swirl butter to evenly coat bottom of skillet. Pour batter into skillet. Bake at 425 degrees for 15 to 18 minutes, until puffy and golden on edges and spots in the center. Remove from oven. Slice and serve, topped with a spoonful of Spiced Fruit and a dusting of powdered sugar. Make 4 to 6 servings.

Spiced Fruit:

2 T. butter
4 apples and/or pears, peeled,
    cored and sliced 1/4-inch
    thick

1/4 c. brown sugar, packed
1 t. cornstarch
1 t. apple pie spice
2 T. lemon juice or water

Melt butter in a skillet over medium-high heat. Add apples or pears; stir until coated with butter. Cook for about 5 minutes, until fruit begins to soften. Stir together remaining ingredients; add to skillet. Cook for another 10 minutes, stirring occasionally, or until fruit is tender and sauce has thickened. Remove from heat; let cool slightly.

If part of a broken eggshell gets into the bowl, just dip in a clean eggshell half. The broken bit will grab onto it like a magnet!

Come Over
for LUNCH

4-H Brunswick Stew

Vivian Marshall
Columbus, OH

This recipe has been in the family for over 70 years. It was a menu item at a 4-H autumn festival that my Aunt Helen was part of in 1949. The festival flyer was saved by my Grandmother Kathleen, and has been in the family ever since. The stew was traditionally made with small game such as squirrel, rabbit and chicken, but we have always used ground beef. It is traditionally served with hot buttered cornbread. We love it...I hope you will too!

2 lbs. lean ground beef
1 c. water
2 onions, chopped
2 c. tomato juice
2 14-1/2 oz. cans lima beans
15-1/4 oz. can corn
4 potatoes, peeled and cubed

2 t. Montreal steak seasoning
1-1/2 t. dried basil
1-1/2 t. paprika
1-1/2 t. garlic salt
cracked pepper to taste
Optional: 1-1/2 t. red pepper
   flakes

Brown beef in a Dutch oven over medium heat; drain. Add water and onions; simmer for 5 minutes. Add tomato juice, undrained beans and undrained corn. Reduce heat to low. Simmer for 1-1/2 hours, stirring occasionally. Add potatoes and simmer until tender, 10 to 15 minutes. Add seasonings as desired; simmer for 15 additional minutes and serve. Makes 10 to 12 servings.

Pass along Grandma's soup tureen or kettle to a
new bride...fill it with favorite seasonings and tie on
a cherished soup recipe.

Come Over for LUNCH

Slow-Cooker Cabbage Soup

Rebecca Wright
Tulsa, OK

*I used to make this soup for my kids when they were growing up...
they still ask for it! It is a wonderful soup, very tasty. I always
serve it with crusty bread or brown & serve rolls.*

14-oz. pkg. smoked pork
   sausage, cut into rounds
2 c. cabbage, chopped, or
   shredded coleslaw mix
2 carrots, peeled and chopped
1 to 2 potatoes, peeled and diced
1 stalk celery, chopped

1/2 onion, diced
15-oz. can diced tomatoes
15-oz. can low-sodium chicken
   broth
1 c. cocktail vegetable juice or
   tomato juice

Combine all ingredients in a 4-quart slow cooker; do not drain tomatoes.
Cover and cook for 6 to 8 hours on low setting, or on high setting for
3 to 4 hours. Makes 6 to 8 servings.

Wide-rimmed soup plates are perfect for serving
hearty dinner portions of soup...perch a warm
buttered roll on the rim!

Grandma's Best
COMFORT FOODS

Grandma's Mex-Can Soup

Daryell Perry
Granby, MO

*This is a super-easy, delicious recipe...it goes together
in a jiffy and everyone loves it.*

1 lb. ground beef
1/2 c. onion, chopped
2 15-1/2 oz. cans black beans,
   drained and rinsed
14-1/2 oz. can diced tomatoes
   with green chiles
15-1/4 oz. can corn
14-1/2 oz. can diced tomatoes
6-oz. can tomato paste
14-1/2 oz. can beef broth

10-1/2 oz. can beef broth
1-1/4 oz. pkg. taco seasoning
   mix
1-oz. pkg. ranch salad dressing
   mix
1/2 t. garlic powder
salt and pepper to taste
Garnish: shredded Cheddar
   cheese, sour cream,
   tortilla chips

In a skillet over medium heat, cook beef with onion until beef is no
longer pink; drain. Add remaining ingredients except garnish; do not
drain tomatoes or corn. Bring to a boil. Reduce heat to medium-low and
simmer for 30 minutes, stirring occasionally. Top with Cheddar cheese
and sour cream; serve with tortilla chips. Makes 8 servings.

To mellow out the sharp taste that tomatoes may have,
stir a teaspoonful of sugar into a simmering pot of soup
or spaghetti sauce.

Come Over
for LUNCH

Mom's Famous Lima Bean Soup
Crystal Vogel
Springdale, PA

Mom always had dinner waiting on the table. I remember coming home from school to a steamy bowl of bean soup that had been simmering for hours on the stove. It's awesome served with warm homemade bread fresh from the oven.

1 lb. cooked ham, cubed
6 c. water
16-oz. pkg. dried baby lima
    beans, rinsed and sorted

1 onion, chopped
1 t. salt
1 t. pepper

Combine ham and water in a stockpot; bring to a boil over medium-high heat. Add remaining ingredients; reduce heat to medium-low. Simmer for about 6 hours, stirring occasionally. Makes 8 to 10 servings.

Mom's Pea Soup
Wendy Jo Minotte
Duluth, MN

No one cooks better than Mom, and this is one of my favorite soups of hers. Goes wonderfully with a thick slice of homemade bread. I hope you enjoy it too!

16-oz. pkg. dried green split
    peas, rinsed and sorted
8 c. water
2-1/2 T. chicken soup base

6 stalks celery, sliced
2 to 3 carrots, peeled and grated
1 c. onion, diced

Add dried peas and water to a soup pot; bring to a boil over medium-high heat. Reduce heat to medium-low; cover and simmer for one to 1-1/2 hours. Stir occasionally, checking to see if peas are soft. Stir in soup base and vegetables. Simmer 15 minutes more. Cool slightly before serving. Serves 6 to 8.

Place onions in the freezer for just 5 minutes, then chop with an extra-sharp knife...no more tears!

Gram's Scotch Broth

Nancy Wise
Little Rock, AR

My grandmother came from Scotland and this was a favorite soup
of hers. It's not spicy, but warm and comforting.

2 lbs. meaty lamb shanks
1 yellow onion, quartered
2 to 3 t. peppercorns
1 c. onion, chopped
1 c. carrots, peeled and chopped
1 c. celery, chopped

1 c. parsnips, peeled and chopped
1 c. turnip, peeled and chopped
1/2 c. quick-cooking pearled
   barley, uncooked
salt and pepper to taste

Combine lamb shanks, onion and peppercorns in a large pot; cover with cold water. Bring to a boil over medium-high heat; skim. Reduce heat to medium-low. Cover and simmer for 2 hours, stirring occasionally. Remove lamb shanks to a plate; cool and chop meat from bones. Strain soup; return to a boil. Add chopped meat, vegetables and barley. Simmer over medium-low heat for one additional hour. Season with salt and pepper before serving. Makes 8 servings.

Seal in the flavor of onions, celery and other soup veggies...
simply sauté them in a little oil before adding broth and
other ingredients.

Grandma Miller's Potato Rolls

*Becky Myers
Ashland, OH*

This is a very old family recipe. My Grandma Miller always made these rolls for every holiday meal, saving the potatoes and their cooking water from dinner the night before. She was born on New Year's Eve in 1902 and began baking at a very early age. She was just the best cook and baker ever! Her original recipe calls for lard, but I always use shortening.

2 baking potatoes, peeled
   and quartered
2/3 c. shortening
2/3 c. sugar

2 eggs, beaten
2-1/2 t. active dry yeast
1 t. salt
7 c. all-purpose flour

In a saucepan over high heat, cover potatoes generously with water. Bring to a boil; cook until potatoes are tender. Drain, reserving 2 cups cooking water; mash potatoes. In a large bowl, combine one cup potatoes, reserved water and remaining ingredients except flour. Stir in flour by cupfuls until dough forms; knead dough until soft. Cover and let dough rise until doubled. Roll out dough on a floured surface; cut dough with a biscuit cutter. Place on parchment paper-lined baking sheets; let rise again. Bake at 350 degrees for about 12 to 15 minutes, until golden. Makes 3 dozen.

Freshen up yesterday's crusty rolls or loaf of bread. Simply sprinkle with water and bake at 400 degrees for 6 to 8 minutes.

Grandma's Best
COMFORT FOODS

Jo's Scale House Soup

Amy Thomason Hunt
Traphill, NC

Our mom was a phenomenal cook. I am originally from West Virginia. Two of my sisters worked at the scale house, where the coal trucks and coal trains were weighed before entering and leaving the tipple with their loads. In the winter, Mom always made vegetable soup for lunch for the people in the office and scale house. I have modified her recipe to use quicker ingredients, but you can use fresh vegetables...it's delicious either way. I can still see Mom making that soup and the guys coming by to pick it up to enjoy on cold and snowy days. I miss her so much, and the good old days of her cooking and the sound of trains and coal trucks passing by.

48-oz. can tomato juice	1/4 t. seasoned salt
1 head cabbage, shredded	1/4 t. salt
3/4 c. onion, diced	1/4 t. pepper
12-oz. can corned beef, finely chopped	1/8 t. red pepper flakes
	2 14-1/4 oz. cans diced potatoes
4 cubes beef bouillon	14-1/4 oz. can mixed vegetables
1/4 t. garlic powder	14-1/4 oz. can lima beans

In a large pot, combine tomato juice, cabbage, onion, corned beef, bouillon cubes and seasonings. Bring to a boil over medium-high heat; reduce heat to medium-low. Simmer for 30 minutes, or until cabbage and onion are tender. Add canned, undrained vegetables; simmer another 15 to 20 minutes, until heated through. Adjust seasonings, as desired. Makes 6 to 8 servings.

What good fortune to grow up in a home
where there are grandparents.
–Suzanne LaFollette

Drop Biscuits

Terri Lotz-Ganley
South Euclid, OH

These homemade biscuits can be served warm with butter and jam or jelly. For a more savory flavor, I'll add one or more additional ingredients, suggested below. They're always delicious!

2 c. all-purpose flour
1 T. baking powder
1 t. salt
Optional: 1 T. sugar
1/2 c. butter, softened

3/4 c. milk
1/4 c. butter, melted
Garnish: additional butter
    for serving

In a large bowl, mix together flour, baking powder, salt and sugar, if desired. Cut in softened butter using a pastry blender, until mixture resembles fine crumbs. Stir in milk until dough leaves the side of the bowl; will be soft and sticky. On a lightly floured surface, gently roll dough in flour to coat. Knead lightly 10 times. Roll out to 1/2-inch thick. Cut with a floured 2-1/2 inch biscuit cutter or the rim of a drinking glass. Place biscuits on an ungreased baking sheet, about one inch apart. Brush lightly with melted butter. Bake at 450 degrees for 10 to 12 minutes, until golden. Immediately remove to a wire rack; serve warm. Makes 10 to 12 biscuits.

Savory biscuit variation: To flour mixture in first step, add 1/3 cup grated Parmesan cheese, shredded sharp Cheddar or Gruyère cheese; 1/3 cup snipped fresh thyme, chives and/or parsley, or one tablespoon lemon zest. Proceed as directed.

Make a fabric liner for a basket of rolls or biscuits...no sewing required! Cut an 18-inch square of homespun and pull away the threads at the edges to create fringes as long as you like.

Grandma's Best COMFORT FOODS

Gram's Not-to-be-Forgotten "Bloney" Sandwiches

Eileen Bennett
Jenison, MI

Beginning with my mother's childhood, a tray of these sandwiches was a tradition for family gatherings. For our annual 4th of July picnic, my job as a kid was to grind the bologna, onion and pickles with an old-fashioned meat grinder. Today, my great-grandchildren are still enjoying these simple-to-make lunchtime treats, and they're still a favorite of my grown-up kids too. I grew up believing this was Gram's original recipe, but I'm told it's a midwestern concoction.

1 lb. ring bologna, skin removed
    and sliced into chunks
1 medium onion, peeled and
    sliced into chunks
1/3 c. sweet pickle relish, or
    finely chopped pickles

1/4 to 1/2 c. mayonnaise,
    divided
buttered sandwich bread
Optional: lettuce leaves

Chop or grind bologna and onion chunks well, using a food processor or grinder. Transfer to a large bowl; add pickle relish. Add mayonnaise, beginning with 1/4 cup; stir to blend. Add remaining mayonnaise to make a spreadable mixture. Cover and refrigerate several hours to blend flavors. To serve, spread on buttered bread to make sandwiches. A lettuce leaf may be added to each sandwich. Makes 8 sandwiches.

To serve hot: Spread bologna mixture on hamburger bun halves. Top with a slice of American cheese. Bake at 350 degrees for several minutes, just until cheese begins to bubble slightly.

To clean an old-fashioned food grinder, just put a half-slice of bread through the grinder as the last item. The bread will remove any food residue in the grinder.

Come Over
for LUNCH

Grandma Beverly's Best-Ever Sloppy Joes

Lorraine Pollachek
Boca Raton, FL

I've eaten these Sloppy Joes since I was a little girl...that's well over 50 years! There are none better than these and I've never used a canned sauce. Serve open-faced over toasted hamburger buns or sliced bread. Also good spooned over hot, crisp French fries or potato puffs, cooked and buttered egg noodles, or with cooked and lightly buttered elbow macaroni stirred in.

2 lbs. ground beef chuck
1 c. onion, diced
2 T. Worcestershire sauce
1 T. granulated garlic
1 t. celery seed
1 t. salt

1/4 t. pepper
1 c. catsup
2 T. mustard
toasted hamburger buns or
 sliced bread

In a large skillet over medium heat, brown beef with onion; crumble well. (Do not drain yet, fat is flavor.) Stir in Worcestershire sauce, garlic and seasonings. Continue cooking for 2 to 3 minutes. Stir in catsup and mustard; reduce heat to medium-low. Cover and simmer for 15 to 30 minutes, stirring occasionally; the longer it simmers, the better it tastes. (May now add more catsup and/or mustard to taste, if desired; simmer longer to blend.) Remove from heat; let stand for 5 minutes. Skim off as much fat from surface as possible; stir well. Spoon over toasted hamburger buns or bread; serve open-faced. Makes 4 to 8 servings.

For an old-fashioned good time, take the family out to a nearby park. While a simple meal cooks on the grill, everyone can swing on the swings, play croquet or just enjoy a hike in the woods. After dinner, make s'mores for dessert... what fun!

Slow-Cooker Taco Soup

Kathleen Bell
Clovis, CA

This warm, tasty soup is easy and comforts your taste buds!
Serve with a basket of saltines or tortilla chips.

1 lb. ground beef
3/4 c. onion, chopped
2 14-1/2 oz. cans diced tomatoes
15-1/4 oz. can corn
15-1/2 oz. can chili beans
15-1/2 oz. can kidney beans
8-oz. can tomato sauce

4-oz. can diced mild green chiles
2 c. water
1-1/4 oz. pkg. taco seasoning
   mix
Garnish: shredded Cheddar
   cheese, sour cream

In a medium skillet, cook and crumble beef with onion until browned. Drain; transfer mixture to a 5-quart slow cooker. Add remaining ingredients except garnish; do not drain any cans. Mix gently to blend. Cover and cook on low setting for 7 to 8 hours, until hot and bubbly. Garnish with shredded cheese and sour cream. Makes 8 servings.

Freeze leftover soup in individual portions to serve later as a soup buffet supper...everyone can choose their favorite! Just add a basket of warm buttered rolls for a cozy, quick & easy meal.

Healthy Lentil Stew

Shirley Howie
Foxboro, MA

This is a vegetarian stew that's very tasty and filling!
I usually serve it with some crusty bread, for a light meal
that is ready in under an hour.

1 c. dried lentils, rinsed
   and sorted
3-1/2 c. chicken broth
14-1/2 oz. can diced tomatoes
1 c. potato, peeled and chopped
1/2 c. celery, chopped

1/2 c. onion, chopped
1/2 c. carrot, peeled and chopped
1 clove garlic, minced
1 T. dried parsley
1 T. dried basil
1/4 t. pepper

Combine lentils, chicken broth, tomatoes with juice and remaining ingredients in a large saucepan over medium-high heat. Bring to a boil; reduce heat to medium-low. Cover and simmer for 45 to 50 minutes, stirring occasionally, until lentils and vegetables are tender. Makes 4 servings.

Store dried beans and rice in canning jars on the kitchen counter for a country charm.

Grandma's Best
COMFORT FOODS

Grandma's Veggie Soup

Dawn McClain
Mascoutah, IL

My mom made this comforting slow-cooker soup for us on cold winter days, just as her mom had done for her. Serve with saltine crackers or cornbread.

2 14-1/2 oz. cans diced tomatoes
10-3/4 oz. can cream of
   mushroom soup
15-1/2 oz. can black beans,
   drained
2 t. honey

1 t. onion powder
1/2 t. cayenne pepper
1 lb. smoked turkey sausage,
   sliced
2 c. potatoes, peeled and diced

In a 5-quart slow cooker, combine tomatoes with juice, mushroom soup, beans, honey and seasonings; stir gently. Add sausage and potatoes; stir together. Cover and cook on low setting for 7 to 8 hours, until bubbly and potatoes are tender. Makes 4 to 6 servings.

Bean & Pasta Soup

Sandy Coffey
Cincinnati, OH

A soup that's fun and different! Add some diced baked ham or hot dogs, if you like.

1 T. butter
1/2 c. onion, chopped
1/2 c. celery, chopped
1/2 c. carrot, peeled and
   shredded
1 clove garlic, minced
10-3/4 oz. can vegetable soup
1-1/4 c. water

15-1/2 oz. can light red kidney
   beans
8-oz. pkg. cavatappi or shell
   pasta, uncooked
1/2 t. dried thyme
1/8 t. pepper
1 bay leaf

Melt butter in a large saucepan over medium heat. Add onion, celery, carrot and garlic; sauté until tender. Stir in remaining ingredients; bring to a boil. Reduce heat to medium-low; simmer until pasta is tender. Discard bay leaf at serving time. Serves 4 to 6.

Turkey Bone Soup

Rebecca Wright
Tulsa, OK

My mother and grandmother used to make this tasty soup after Thanksgiving...it was my favorite part of the leftovers. I serve it with a crusty bread.

1 meaty turkey carcass
6 c. water
1 to 2 potatoes, peeled and
   chopped
1 to 2 carrots, peeled and
   chopped

1 to 2 stalks celery, chopped
2 t. poultry seasoning
8-oz. pkg. broad egg noodles,
   uncooked
1 c. frozen peas

In a soup pot, cover turkey carcass with water. Bring to a boil over high heat; reduce heat to medium-low and simmer for 30 minutes. Remove carcass to a platter. Strain broth in pot and add 4 to 5 cups broth to a 5-quart slow cooker. Add potatoes, carrots, celery and seasoning. When cool enough to handle, pick turkey off bones and add to broth, discarding bones. Cover and cook on low setting for 7 to 8 hours, or on high setting for 3 to 4 hours. About 30 minutes before soup is done, add noodles and peas; cover and finish cooking. Makes 8 to 10 servings.

Cute-as-a-button kitchen magnets! Look through Grandma's button box to choose a variety of buttons. Hot-glue each button to a small magnet, and it's ready to keep recipes and shopping lists handy on the fridge.

Creamy Corn & Sausage Soup

Joyce Roebuck
Jacksonville, TX

This is a really good soup on a cold winter evening...
it warms the soul.

1 lb. smoked pork sausage, diced
1 c. onion, chopped
2 c. water
3 potatoes, peeled and diced
1 T. fresh parsley, chopped
1 t. dried basil

2 t. salt
1/8 t. pepper
15-1/2 oz. can corn
14-3/4 oz. can cream-style corn
1-1/2 c. evaporated milk

Brown sausage in a large skillet over medium heat. Drain, reserving 2 tablespoons drippings in pan. Add onion and sauté until soft. Stir in water, potatoes, parsley and seasonings. Cover and simmer for 45 minutes. Stir in undrained corn, cream-style corn and evaporated milk; cover and heat just to boiling. Makes 4 to 6 servings.

The ultimate comfort food...place a scoop of mashed
potatoes in the center of a soup bowl, then ladle
hearty stew all around.

Mom's Easy Chili

Vicky Feldman
Greensburg, IN

This recipe was my mother's old standby for a chilly night. She worked full-time and this was quick to toss together. It is still one of my favorite comfort foods and reminds me of her...it is a favorite of my children as well. Serve with oyster crackers or cornbread with butter and honey, and a big glass of cold milk!

1 lb. ground beef
Optional: chopped onion, green
  pepper to taste
1 to 2 10-3/4 oz. cans tomato
  soup
2 15-1/2 oz. cans mild or hot
  chili beans

15-1/2 oz. can kidney beans
  w/juice
chili powder to taste
2 to 3 T. sugar, to taste
Optional: 1-1/4 c. water

Brown beef in a Dutch oven over medium heat, adding onion and green peppers if desired. Drain; stir in tomato soup and undrained beans. Season with chili powder and sugar to taste. If chili is too thick, stir in water. Simmer over medium-low heat for 10 to 20 minutes to blend flavors. Makes 6 to 8 servings.

Crunchy toppings can really add fun and flavor to chili and
soup. Fill a muffin tin with some fun and tasty choices...
fish–shaped crackers, bacon bits, French fried onions,
sunflower seeds and toasted nuts.

Grandma's Best COMFORT FOODS

Rachel's Tuna Bunsteads

Elaine Divis
Sioux City, IA

This has been a family favorite for three generations! Grandma Rachel often made these sandwiches when we'd gather to cheer on our Iowa Hawkeyes football team. Go Hawks!

3 eggs, hard-boiled, peeled
    and diced
2 c. shredded Co-Jack, Cheddar
    or pasteurized process cheese
7-oz. can tuna, drained and
    flaked
2 T. onion, finely diced

2 T. green pepper, finely diced
2 T. green olives with pimentos,
    sliced
2 T. sweet pickle relish
1/2 c. mayonnaise
8 hot dog buns, split

In a large bowl, combine all ingredients except buns; mix well. Spoon mixture into hot dog buns; place on an ungreased baking sheet. Bake at 300 degrees for about 30 minutes, until cheese is melted and buns are toasty. Makes 8 sandwiches.

Just for fun, serve soda pop in vintage glass bottles alongside a casual soup & sandwich meal.

Come Over
for LUNCH

Wimpy Sandwich

Christy Smith
Grove City, PA

My mom always made these sandwiches when time was short. She named them after the comic strip character from her childhood who would "gladly pay you tomorrow for a hamburger today."

1 lb. ground beef
1/2 c. yellow onion, diced
4 to 6 slices American cheese
1/2 t. mustard

1/2 t. Worcestershire sauce
4 to 5 slices white bread, toasted
   if desired

Brown beef in a skillet over medium heat. Drain, reserving a small amount of drippings in pan. Add onion and cook until translucent. Add cheese slices to beef mixture; stir until melted. Stir in mustard and Worcestershire sauce. Spoon onto bread or toast slices and serve. Makes 4 to 5 open-faced sandwiches.

Grandma Cook's Grilled Tomato Toasties

Brenda Huey
Geneva, IN

My Grandma Cook made these often when I visited her for lunch. My dad and his brothers worked across the road at the feed mill. We would walk over to Grandma's for lunch and fix these sandwiches.

4 slices bread
softened butter to taste

1 ripe tomato, sliced
2 slices favorite cheese

Spread both sides of bread slices with butter. Lay 2 slices on a hot griddle over medium heat; top each with sliced tomato and a slice of cheese. Add remaining bread and cook until golden on both sides. Makes 2 sandwiches.

A smiling face is half the meal.
–Latvian proverb

Mom's Date-Nut Bread

Judy Henfey
Cibolo, TX

My mom belonged to a Ladies' Grange back in the 70s and she'd bake this bread when having coffee with friends. This recipe came from an old Grange cookbook. I call this my "antique" recipe because you don't often see Date Bread baked anymore. I've recently rediscovered dates and I think you should too. Happy memories!

8-oz. pkg. chopped dates	1 t. baking powder
1-1/2 c. boiling water	1 t. baking soda
2 T. butter	1 t. salt
1-1/2 c. light or dark brown sugar, packed	1 egg, lightly beaten
	1 t. vanilla extract
2-1/2 c. all-purpose flour	1 c. walnuts, finely chopped

In a bowl, cover dates with boiling water; add butter and set aside to cool. Add brown sugar and stir well. In another bowl, sift together flour, baking powder, baking soda and salt. Add date mixture and egg to flour mixture; stir well. Add vanilla and walnuts; mix well. Pour batter into a greased 9"x5" loaf pan. Bake at 350 degrees for one hour and 10 to 15 minutes. Cool and slice. Makes one loaf.

Bake Mom's Date-Nut Bread in mini loaves to give as gifts.
Wrap individually in colored cellophane, tea towels or
just tie a ribbon around the loaf pan!

Come Over
for LUNCH

Comforting Chicken Noodle Soup

Donna Reeter
Vandalia, IL

This recipe was given to me by a dear friend, who was about 87 at the time she gave it to me. The soup is just what the name says... comforting, creamy and delicious. This recipe may be cut in half for small families or a couple.

8 c. water
8 cubes chicken bouillon
6-1/2 c. wide egg noodles, uncooked
3 c. cooked chicken, cubed

2 10-3/4 oz. cans cream of chicken soup
8-oz. container sour cream
Optional: chopped fresh parsley

In a large soup pot, bring water and bouillon cubes to a boil over high heat. Add noodles; cook according to package instructions, until tender. Do not drain. Stir in chicken and chicken soup; heat through. Remove from heat; stir in sour cream. Sprinkle with parsley, if desired. Makes 10 to 12 servings.

A pot of chicken soup and a cheery bouquet of posies
are sure pick-me-ups for a friend who is feeling
under the weather.

Irene's Corn Chowder

Doreen Knapp
Stanfordville, NY

This is my Auntie Irene's recipe. She lived in Connecticut and used to cook for the Retired Armed Forces Association. All the guys would come for my aunt's great and eclectic soups. I have tons of her soup recipes...miss her so much.

1/2 c. butter, sliced
1 c. onion, chopped
1 c. celery, diced
4 c. chicken or vegetable broth
3 to 4 potatoes, peeled and diced
1/4 t. salt
1/2 t. pepper

2 14-3/4 oz. cans cream-style corn
12-oz. pkg. frozen corn
3 to 4 c. milk
Garnish: 4 slices crisply cooked, crumbled bacon

Melt butter in a soup pot over medium heat. Add onion and celery; sauté for about 10 minutes. Add chicken or vegetable broth, potatoes, salt and pepper. Simmer over low heat for 10 to 15 minutes, until potatoes are almost knife-tender. Add cream-style corn and frozen corn; stir well. Add 3 cups milk; check consistency and add remaining cup of milk, if desired. Cook until heated through; simmer for another 5 to 7 minutes. Serve topped with crumbled bacon. Makes 6 servings.

Chicken backs and wings are excellent for making rich, delicious broth...a terrific way to use up the last of farm-raised fowl. Save up unused ones in the freezer until you have enough for a pot of broth.

Come Over
for LUNCH

Tomato-Wine Soup

Wendy Meadows
Spring Hill, FL

This was one of my Great-Grandmother Krupa's recipes. The last time I had it, I was seven years old. She made it for my cousins, sister and me along with grilled cheese sandwiches to warm us up after a day playing in the snow.

2 c. ripe tomatoes or canned
    whole peeled tomatoes
1/4 c. butter
2 T. all-purpose flour
1 T. fresh basil, snipped
1 t. fresh thyme, snipped

1 t. salt
1/8 t. pepper
1/4 t. baking soda
1 c. half-and-half
1/2 c. dry white wine or water

If using fresh tomatoes, chop; simmer in a saucepan with butter until soft. Cool and purée or blend until smooth; return to saucepan. If using canned tomatoes, blend in blender and add to saucepan along with butter. Stir in flour, herbs, salt and pepper. Bring to a boil over medium-high heat. Reduce heat to medium-low; simmer for 5 minutes. Stir in baking soda and half-and-half. Cook over low heat until slightly thickened; do not boil. Stir in wine or water and heat to a simmer. Makes 4 small servings.

Nothing perks up the flavor of tomato sauce like fresh basil!
Grandma probably had some in her garden, but if you don't have
a garden, keep a pot of basil in the kitchen windowsill. Just
pinch off a few leaves whenever they're needed.

Grandma's Best
COMFORT FOODS

Gram's Chili for a Crowd

Katherine Nelson
Centerville, UT

I love this slow-cooker recipe because it tastes like the chili I love from a favorite fast-food restaurant. It's especially great for a large group. Spices can be adjusted to your taste. I love to serve this with a sweet cornbread.

2 lbs. ground beef
29-oz. can kidney beans
29-oz. can pinto beans
14-1/2 oz. can petite diced
    tomatoes
2 c. water
29-oz. can tomato sauce

2 4-oz. cans diced green chiles
1 c. onion, diced
1/4 c. celery, diced
3 T. chili powder, or to taste
2 t. ground cumin
2 t. salt
1-1/2 t. pepper

Brown beef in a large skillet over medium heat; drain. Transfer beef to a 6-quart slow cooker; add undrained beans, undrained tomatoes and remaining ingredients. Cover and cook on high setting for 4 hours. Add more water if needed as it cooks, to make it the desired thickness. Makes 12 to 14 servings.

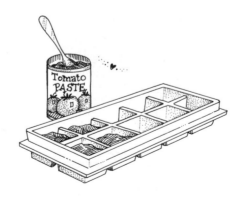

A spoonful of tomato paste adds rich flavor to soups and roasts. If you have a partial can left over, freeze the rest in an ice cube tray, then store cubes in a freezer bag. Frozen cubes can be dropped right into simmering dishes.

Come Over
for LUNCH

Grandmother's Buttermilk Cornbread

*Kim Duncan
Sellersburg, IN*

This cornbread brings back so many memories of my dear grandmother. She would make it in her cast-iron skillet, and I couldn't wait for it to come out of the oven. With a big pat of butter on top, it's total comfort food!

1 T. bacon drippings or olive oil	1/8 t. baking soda
1-3/4 c. buttermilk	1 c. all-purpose flour
1/4 c. olive oil	1 c. cornmeal
1 T. baking powder	1 t. salt

Add bacon drippings or olive oil to a cast-iron skillet; place in a 450-degree oven to heat. Meanwhile, in a large bowl, combine remaining ingredients and mix well. Spoon batter into hot skillet, adding a spoonful in the center. (This will make it easy to cut or break into serving pieces.) Bake at 450 degrees for 20 to 25 minutes, until golden. Cut into wedges or squares. Makes 6 to 8 servings.

Cut flowers in a canning jar are so cheerful on the dinner table. Whether they're from your backyard garden or the grocery store, keep them blooming longer...add a teaspoon of sugar and 1/2 teaspoon of household bleach to the water in the jar.

Vegetable Chowder

*Wendy Lee Paffenroth
Pine Island, NY*

*Good for lunch on a rainy Saturday! My mom loved her chowders.
This is one she made until age 93, when she had to give up her
home and stop cooking. Serve with warm biscuits.*

2 T. butter
2 c. cabbage, chopped
1 c. onion, chopped
1 c. celery, chopped
1 c. carrots, peeled and
   thinly sliced
2 14-1/2 oz. cans chicken broth
12-oz. pkg. frozen sweet peas

15-1/4 oz. can cream-style corn
2 to 3 c. whole or 2% milk
8-oz. pkg. shredded or sliced
   mild Cheddar cheese, to
   desired consistency
1 t. fresh parsley, chopped
1/8 t. celery seed
salt and pepper to taste

Melt butter in a heavy stockpot over medium heat. Sauté cabbage and
onion until translucent. Add celery, carrots and chicken broth; bring to
a boil. Add peas and corn. Stir in milk; bring to a simmer. Add desired
amount of cheese; cook and stir until melted. Add seasonings; heat
through, stirring often, but do not boil. Serves 8.

Grandma was sure to have several cans of evaporated milk
tucked in the pantry. It adds a creamy touch to milk-based
soups and it's easy to keep on hand, since it needs
no refrigeration.

Come Over for LUNCH

Grandma Mary's Irish Bread

Michelle Geraghty
Whitman, MA

My mother-in-law shared this recipe with me years ago. It was her mother's recipe. I like to use a springform pan, but you can do as she did and bake it in an oven-safe skillet. It is not your typical Irish soda bread with caraway, which is what I love about it. She has since passed, but we honor her every Saint Patrick's Day...and other holidays too. Enjoy with a nice cup of tea!

10 T. butter, softened and
   divided
4 c. all-purpose flour
4 t. baking powder
1 t. baking soda

1/2 t. salt
2 T. cinnamon
1/3 c. sugar
2-1/3 c. milk, divided
1 c. raisins

Coat a 2" deep 10" springform or oven-proof straight-sided skillet with 2 tablespoons butter; set aside. In a bowl, whisk together flour, baking powder, baking soda, salt and cinnamon; set aside. In a large bowl, beat together 6 tablespoons butter and sugar until well blended. Add half of milk and mix well; add half of flour mixture and mix well. Repeat with milk and flour mixture. Fold in raisins and spread batter into prepared pan. Bake at 350 degrees for 45 to 50 minutes, or until a toothpick tests clean, checking after 40 minutes. Immediately spread remaining butter over bread; let stand in pan for 15 minutes. Turn bread out of skillet or loosen the springform sides; let cool before cutting. Makes one loaf.

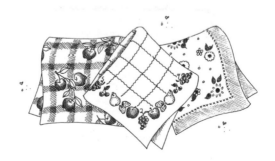

Vintage cotton tea towels are so handy in the kitchen for drying freshly rinsed vegetables, covering a bowl of bread dough and much more. They're reusable too...much thriftier than paper towels!

Fred's Fish Stew

Gloria Huse
Simpsonville, SC

This beloved family recipe belonged to my husband's great-grandfather, Fred Holder, Sr. His great-grandparents loved being at the lake, as we do, and were always cooking up big meals that included fish. I have this recipe in his own handwriting framed at our lake house, as do many other family members of his. I have modified the recipe to make it easy for others to follow. At the end of the recipe, Fred wrote, "Eat all you can hold and then put a little in each pocket." Enjoy!

3 lbs. boneless freshwater bass,
    crappie or catfish fillets
3 c. potatoes, peeled and chopped
3 c. onions, chopped
2 to 4 c. water

2 to 4 c. milk
15-1/4 oz. can corn, drained
3/4 c. butter, sliced
1 t. salt, or to taste
1/2 t. pepper, or to taste

In a large boiler or cooking pot, combine fish fillets, potatoes and onions with enough water to cover. Cook over medium heat until vegetables are soft; drain. Add desired amount of milk and remaining ingredients. Simmer over medium-low heat until soup comes to a boil, stirring often; serve. Makes 10 servings.

For mild, fresh-tasting frozen fish, place frozen fillets in
a shallow dish, cover with milk and let thaw overnight
in the fridge.

Mom's Potato Soup

Deanna Adams
Garland, TX

This was my mom's recipe, which I've made and embellished over the years. It remains a family favorite. This is nice as a first course or as part of a ladies' lunch.

5 lbs. russet potatoes, peeled and cut into 1-inch cubes
1 c. white or yellow onion, diced
2 to 3 stalks celery, diced
Optional: 1 to 2 carrots, peeled and diced
2 to 3 c. chicken broth or water

2 c. half-and-half or milk
salt and pepper to taste
Garnish: sour cream, shredded Cheddar cheese, finely chopped green onions or chives, bacon bits

Combine vegetables in a large soup pot or Dutch oven. Add chicken broth or water; liquid should cover vegetables. Bring to a boil over medium-high heat. Reduce heat to medium-low and simmer until vegetables are tender, about 20 minutes. Mash vegetables slightly, if desired. Stir in half-and-half or milk; season with salt and pepper. Bring to a simmer; cook for 10 minutes. Serve hot, with garnishes on the side for each person to add. Serves 4 to 6.

Chilled variation: Allow soup to cool to room temperature; cover and refrigerate. Serve chilled, topped with a dollop of sour cream and a sprinkle of chopped chives.

Soups and stews are easy to stretch when you need to feed
a few more people. Just add a few more chopped veggies
and a little more broth or cream, then simmer until done...
no one will know the difference!

Applesauce Spice Bread

Rebecca Etling
Blairsville, PA

A scrumptious recipe for fall...the whole house smells delicious when it's baking!

1-1/4 c. applesauce
1 c. sugar
1/2 c. oil
2 eggs, beaten
3 T. milk
2 c. all-purpose flour

1/2 t. baking powder
1 t. baking soda
1-1/2 t. cinnamon
1 t. nutmeg
1/4 t. allspice

In a large bowl, combine applesauce, sugar, oil, eggs and milk; mix well. In a separate bowl, sift together remaining ingredients. Stir flour mixture into applesauce mixture; beat well. Divide batter between 2 greased 9"x5" loaf pans; sprinkle Topping over batter. Bake at 350 degrees for 45 minutes, or until a toothpick inserted in the center comes out clean. Makes 2 loaves.

Topping:

1/4 c. brown sugar

1 t. cinnamon

Combine ingredients; mix well.

Enjoy a warm muffin anytime! Extra muffins can be wrapped in aluminum foil and kept in the freezer for up to a month. To serve, reheat at 300 degrees for 15 to 18 minutes.

Aunt Nancy's Cream of Parisian Soup

Lisa Burns
Findlay, OH

This is such a great soup that my Aunt Nancy used to make...it just warms the belly! Serve it with a crisp salad and a slice of bread and butter. The ham is definitely optional, but oh-so good.

16-oz. pkg. frozen broccoli,
    cauliflower and carrots
1/2 c. butter
1/2 c. margarine
1/2 c. celery, chopped
1/2 c. onion, chopped
1 c. all-purpose flour

4 cubes chicken bouillon,
    crushed, or 4 t. chicken
    bouillon granules
6 c. milk
Optional: 1 c. cooked ham, diced
salt and pepper to taste

In a large saucepan, cook vegetables according to package directions; do not drain. Meanwhile, in another saucepan, melt butter with margarine over medium heat. Add celery and onion; sauté until onion is translucent. Add flour and stir until blended. Add bouillon cubes and milk; stir until smooth. Add cooked vegetables with their cooking liquid; add ham, if desired. Season with salt and pepper; heat through and serve. Makes 3 quarts.

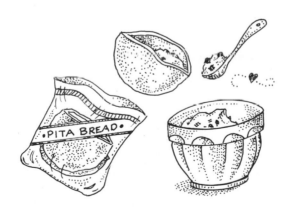

Round out a soup supper with some tasty egg sandwiches!
Simply scramble eggs to your taste and serve in pita halves
or on toasted English muffins.

Easiest–Ever Chicken
& Dumplings

Kristy Wells
Ocala, FL

My Mamaw made the best chicken & dumplings from scratch, but when she tried to teach me, I could never get the recipe right. She had a wonderful old-school way of cooking and measuring. Her recipe called for 3 fingers of grease, 2 handfuls of flour and enough milk or water to make it stick. She has since passed on and her dumplings are only a heartfelt memory, so I came up with this substitute that I hope your family enjoys as much as mine. Mamaw liked to add baby lima beans for extra flavor.

2 lbs. chicken breasts
1 c. carrots, peeled and chopped
1 c. celery, chopped
1/2 c. onion, chopped
1 to 2 T. poultry seasoning

7-1/2 oz. tube refrigerated
    biscuits, cut into half-inch
    pieces
salt and pepper to taste

Add chicken to a large soup pot; cover with water. Bring to a boil over medium-high heat; simmer until chicken is cooked through. Remove chicken to a platter to cool, reserving broth in pot. Add vegetables and poultry seasoning; return to a boil. Pull chicken off bones and add, discarding skin and bones. Simmer until vegetables are crisp-tender. Drop biscuit pieces into soup, adding a little water if biscuits aren't covered by broth. Return to a rolling boil. Cook until dumplings are cooked through, about 10 minutes. At serving time, season with salt and pepper. Serves 6 to 8.

A sprinkle of fresh herbs can make a good soup even better. Some good choices are parsley, basil, oregano and thyme. For the freshest flavor, stir in herbs about 20 minutes before the soup is done.

Hamburger Soup

Bev Traxler
British Columbia, Canada

This soup is a great hit with the kids and grandkids. Feel free to use a variety of favorite vegetables. It also freezes well. Serve with rolls or buns.

1-1/2 lbs. ground beef
3/4 c. onion, finely chopped
28-oz. can crushed tomatoes
2 c. water
3 10-1/2 oz. cans beef
   consommé or broth
10-3/4 oz. can tomato soup

4 carrots, peeled and finely
   chopped
3 stalks celery, finely chopped
1/2 c. pearled barley, uncooked
salt and pepper to taste
1 bay leaf

Brown beef with onion in a soup pot over medium heat; drain well. Add remaining ingredients. Cover and simmer over medium-low heat at least 2 hours or all day, stirring occasionally. Remove bay leaf before serving. May also use a slow cooker; combine all ingredients and cook on low setting for 6 to 8 hours, until vegetables are tender. Makes 10 servings.

Homemade soup often tastes even better if made a day ahead and refrigerated overnight. It's a snap to skim any fat too... it will solidify on the surface and can easily be spooned off.

Beckie's Biscuit Rolls

Beckie Apple
Grannis, AR

My mother taught me to make and bake biscuits when I was ten years old...that was more than 50 years ago! Since my husband of 40-plus years loves homemade bread, I have had lots of practice. This bread recipe is really a cross between a biscuits and a hot roll and is a good complement to any meal.

1-3/4 c. buttermilk
1 T. fast-rising yeast
3 T. sugar, divided
2-1/4 c. self-rising flour

1 T. baking powder
5 T. cold margarine, sliced
    and divided
1 t. oil

In a microwave-safe glass measuring cup, microwave buttermilk for one minute. Add yeast and 2 tablespoons sugar; stir until yeast is well mixed. Let stand for 5 minutes. Meanwhile, in a bowl, combine flour, baking powder and remaining sugar; mix well. Add 4 tablespoons sliced margarine. Using a pastry blender or your fingers, mix margarine into flour until it resembles coarse meal. Add buttermilk mixture and stir well; dough will be somewhat tight. Add oil to bowl; turn dough in bowl to coat with oil. Cover bowl with plastic wrap; set in a cold oven or microwave. Let rise for one hour. Place dough on a floured surface; work dough for one to 2 minutes. Form dough into an oblong roll. Pinch off dough to form 10 to 12 balls, each 3 inches in diameter. Arrange in a lightly oiled 9"x9" baking pan. Top each ball with a small slice of remaining margarine; return to cold oven or microwave to rise for one more hour. Bake at 400 degrees for 15 to 18 minutes, until golden. Makes 10 to 12 biscuits.

Treat everyone to honey-pecan butter with warm biscuits or rolls. Simply blend together 1/2 cup butter, 1/2 cup honey and 1/3 cup toasted chopped pecans. Delectable!

Grandma's Best
SIDES & SALADS

Southern Potato Salad

Sherri Hagymas
Londonderry, NH

I grew up on my grandmother's southern-style potato salad and for the longest time, I never had a true recipe for it. She just tossed in some ingredients and did a taste test. I'm thrilled that I finally mastered it!

2 lbs. potatoes, peeled and
    cut into 1-inch cubes
7 eggs
1 c. mayonnaise

1 t. mustard
1/4 c. sweet pickle relish
salt and pepper to taste

In a large saucepan over high heat, cover potatoes with water; bring to a boil. Cook for about 15 minutes, until tender. Drain potatoes in a colander; transfer to a bowl and refrigerate for about one hour. (This keeps potatoes from crumbling.) Meanwhile, in another large saucepan over high heat, cover eggs with water. Bring to a boil; reduce heat to low and simmer, uncovered, for one minute. Remove from heat; cover and let stand for 20 minutes. Peel, slice and dice eggs. In a large bowl, mix together remaining ingredients. Add potatoes and eggs; mix gently. Serves 8.

Potatoes come in 3 basic types. Round waxy potatoes are excellent in potato salads, soups and casseroles. Starchy russet potatoes bake up fluffy and are great for frying too. All-purpose potatoes are in between and work well in most recipes. Do some delicious experimenting to find your favorites!

Grandma's Best
SIDES & SALADS

Aunt Ella's Bean Salad

Theresa Wehmeyer
Rosebud, MO

My husband's Aunt Ella always brought this delicious bean salad to family gatherings. It remains a favorite at our house. It is great to take to outdoor summer gatherings, since the dressing is not mayonnaise-based.

15-1/2 oz. can kidney beans, drained and rinsed
14-1/2 oz. can green beans, drained
14-1/2 oz. can yellow beans
2 green onions, finely chopped

1/2 c. red pepper, diced
3/4 c. sugar
2/3 c. white vinegar
1/2 c. oil
1 t. salt
1/2 t. pepper, or to taste

Combine kidney beans and green beans in a serving bowl. Add yellow beans with liquid from can. Add green onions and red pepper; set aside. In a separate bowl, mix together sugar, vinegar and oil; stir to dissolve sugar. Add salt and pepper. Pour mixture over vegetables; toss to coat. Cover and refrigerate for 24 hours before serving. Stir again at serving time. Makes 10 servings.

Blue Willow is a classic vintage china pattern...why not start a collection of pieces from tag sales and thrift shops? Whether they're fine porcelain or treasures from a yard sale, your mix & match finds are sure to blend together.

Grandma's Best
COMFORT FOODS

Mother's Junk Salad

Janae Mallonee
Marlboro, MA

Growing up, I had no idea there was any kind of macaroni salad other than this one! My mother and all of my aunties made it the same way. As I have branched out and tried new salads, I like them too, but nothing ever compares to this old faithful.

16-oz. pkg. elbow macaroni,
    uncooked
1 c. mayonnaise
6-oz. can tuna, drained
    and flaked
2 tomatoes, diced

1 cucumber, diced
1 green pepper, diced
4 dill pickle spears, diced
1/4 c. dill pickle juice
Italian seasoning, garlic powder
    and pepper to taste

Cook macaroni according to package directions; drain. Rinse with cold water; drain and add to a large bowl. Add remaining ingredients except seasonings; mix well. Add seasonings as desired. Cover and chill until serving time. Makes 8 to 10 servings as a side dish, or 6 to 8 servings as a main dish.

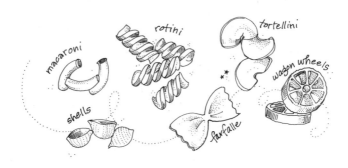

Try using a different shape of pasta in a favorite recipe for macaroni salad. Wagon wheels, seashells and bowties all work well...and they're fun for kids too!

Grandma's Best
SIDES & SALADS

Grandma's Vintage Salad

Marla Kinnersley
Surprise, AZ

This is one of the first recipes Grandma and I would make together in the kitchen. It is really good and has stood the test of time for all of us. We like it as a side salad.

1 head iceberg lettuce, chopped
1 c. seedless red grapes,
   quartered
1 apple, cored and chopped
2 stalks celery, chopped

1/2 c. chopped walnuts
1/4 c. red onion, chopped
6 T. mayonnaise-style salad
   dressing

Combine all ingredients in a large bowl, folding in salad dressing last. Serve immediately. Makes 4 to 6 servings.

Garden Lettuce Salad

Margaret Welder
Madrid, IA

My mother used to make this salad in the springtime, using Black Simpson seed lettuce. It was so quick and tasty. She was an excellent cook and knew how to improvise with what she had on hand.

4 c. leaf lettuce, torn
1/2 sweet onion, thinly sliced
1/2 c. regular or light sour cream
3 T. sugar

2 t. cider vinegar
1/4 t. salt
1/8 t. pepper

In a large bowl, toss lettuce with onion; set aside. In another bowl, combine remaining ingredients; spoon over lettuce and toss to coat lettuce. Serve soon after adding dressing. Serves 4.

If I had known how wonderful it
would be to have grandchildren,
I'd have had them first.
–Lois Wyse

71

Grandma's Best COMFORT FOODS

Southwestern Baked Corn Scallop

Delores Lakes
Mansfield, OH

One of my sweet mother's recipes! She was a good cook and grew up in a family of excellent cooks...just good comfort food.

14-3/4 oz. can cream-style corn
2 eggs, lightly beaten
3/4 c. milk
1/2 c. saltine crackers, coarsely crushed
1 T. canned chopped green chiles

1 t. sugar
3/4 t. salt
1/8 t. pepper
1 c. shredded sharp Cheddar cheese

Combine all ingredients in a bowl; mix well. Transfer to a greased one-quart casserole dish. Bake, uncovered, at 350 degrees for one hour, or until bubbly and golden. Makes 6 to 8 servings.

Why not choose comfort foods as the theme of your next potluck at church or school? What fun to sample everyone else's idea of comfort...and everything is sure to be scrumptious!

Grandma's Best
SIDES & SALADS

Mother-in-Law's Barbecue Potatoes

Gladys Kielar
Whitehouse, OH

My mother-in-law gave me her recipes when she no longer cooked. This is one of our favorites...we hope your family enjoys it too.

4 baking potatoes, each cut
    lengthwise into 8 wedges
1/4 c. butter, melted
3 T. catsup

1 t. brown sugar, packed
1 t. chili powder
1/8 t. salt
1/8 t. cayenne pepper

Arrange potato wedges in a greased 13"x9" baking pan; set aside. In a small bowl, combine remaining ingredients; brush some of sauce over potatoes. Bake at 425 degrees for 30 minutes, or until potatoes are tender, brushing occasionally with remaining sauce. Makes 4 servings.

Ripe red tomatoes and sweet onions from the garden are such a treat in summer. Serve them simply, with just a dash of oil & vinegar and a sprinkle of fresh basil.

Grandma's Best
COMFORT FOODS

Grandma Slovan's Mac & Cheese
Molly Lyons
Columbus, OH

When it came to food, my Grandma Slovan knew what she was doing! This recipe in particular is one of my favorites. When I was young, I knew that if I stayed home from school "sick" I would get to go over to her house, eat mac & cheese until my belly was full and play "Go Fish" for hours on end. This is now a weekly staple side dish in my house!

16-oz. pkg. elbow macaroni,
    uncooked
1/2 c. butter
1 c. milk

16-oz. pkg. pasteurized process
    cheese, cubed
salt and pepper to taste

Cook macaroni according to package directions; drain and set aside. Meanwhile, melt butter in a large saucepan over medium heat; add milk and cheese. Cook, stirring constantly, until well mixed and cheese is melted. Season with salt and pepper. Add cooked macaroni and stir until completely mixed. Serves 6 to 8.

Grandma Hodges' Baked Beans
Becky Bosen
Syracuse, UT

My grandma was an amazing cook. She brought her famous baked beans to all of our family's summertime parties. She's been gone for many years now, but her simple recipe lives on in our family and is always a gentle reminder of her.

1/2 lb. bacon
3/4 c. onion, diced
3 15-oz. cans pork & beans

1 c. brown sugar, packed
3/4 c. catsup

In a large skillet over medium heat, cook bacon with onion until bacon is crisp. Drain; crumble bacon and return to pan. Stir in remaining ingredients; transfer to a greased 13"x9" baking pan. Bake, uncovered, at 375 degrees for 45 to 50 minutes. Serves 8 to 10.

Grandma's Best
SIDES & SALADS

Crispy Soft Oven-Roasted Country Potatoes

Charlene Barbier
Covington, LA

This recipe comes from my grandma's kitchen. She shared her recipes with me when I got married. Whenever I make these potatoes, I can still feel my grandma's love. She left a legacy of good home cooking... thank you, Bammaw.

10 new redskin potatoes,
   quartered
1 T. olive oil

2 T. butter, melted
1 t. herb seasoning blend
1 t. paprika

Place quartered potatoes in a 13"x9" baking pan sprayed with non-stick vegetable spray. Drizzle with olive oil and melted butter; stir to coat potatoes. Sprinkle with seasonings. Bake, uncovered, at 350 degrees for one hour, or until potatoes are crisp on the outside and soft inside. Makes 4 servings.

Check out a nearby farmers' market for seasonal, locally grown vegetables, fruit and herbs. It's a great place to save on fresh-picked produce...you may even discover a new favorite!

Baked Curried Fruit

Linda Shively
Hopkinsville, KY

*This casserole smells almost as good as it tastes! My mom loved
to serve this with roast turkey and baked ham dinners. It's very
pretty and wonderful when served while warm.*

20-oz. can pineapple chunks
15-1/4 oz. can apricot halves
15-1/4 oz. can pear halves
15-1/4 oz. can peach halves
Optional: 10-oz. jar maraschino
    cherries, drained

3/4 c. light brown sugar, packed
1/3 c. butter, sliced
1 t. curry powder

Drain all fruits into a bowl; reserve 1-1/2 cups of juice. Add fruit
mixture to a lightly greased 13"x9" baking pan; set aside. In a saucepan,
combine reserved fruit juice, brown sugar, butter and curry powder.
Cook over medium-low heat until butter is melted and brown sugar is
dissolved. Pour juice mixture over fruit; stir to mix. Bake, uncovered,
at 350 degrees for one hour, until heated through. Serve warm.
Serves 8 to 10.

Keep a stash of aprons in big and little sizes for everyone
who wants to help out in the kitchen.

Kansas Corn Salad

Evangeline Boston
Bradley Junction, FL

Back in 2001, I asked a Kansas City restaurant employee for the ingredients of this great salad. She told me the ingredients and I made it as I liked it. The restaurant is long gone, but the salad is still a favorite.

16-oz. pkg. frozen corn, thawed
3/4 c. onion, chopped

1 green or red pepper, chopped
1 or 2 firm tomatoes, chopped

Combine all vegetables in a large bowl. Pour Dressing over vegetables; mix gently and taste, adding more mayonnaise if needed to make it creamy. Serves 8.

Dressing:

1 c. mayonnaise, or more
    as needed
1/4 c. Italian salad dressing

2 to 3 t. sugar, to taste
salt and pepper to taste

Mix all ingredients well.

Serve up a veggie plate for dinner...a good old Southern tradition.
With 2 or 3 scrumptious veggie dishes and a basket of
buttery cornbread, no one will miss the meat!

Uncle Ron's Perfection Salad

Janis Parr
Ontario, Canada

This was my husband's uncle's recipe. He made this scrumptious salad for every family celebration, always served in a large clear crystal bowl to show off the pretty colors. It's sweet and tangy and has remained a favorite in our family through four generations.

4 envs. unflavored gelatin
1 c. cold water
2 c. boiling water
1-1/2 c. sugar
1/2 c. white vinegar
juice of 1 lemon
1 t. salt

Optional: few drops green food
   coloring
1-1/2 c. cabbage, finely shredded
1-1/2 c. celery, finely chopped
2 carrots, peeled and finely
   shredded

Combine gelatin and cold water in a small bowl; let stand for 5 minutes. In a large bowl, combine boiling water, sugar, vinegar, lemon juice and salt. Add food coloring, if desired. Add gelatin and stir well. Transfer to a 13"x9" glass baking pan. Refrigerate until partially set. Add cabbage, celery and carrot; stir well to combine. Cover and refrigerate until completely set. Makes 6 to 8 servings.

Gelatin salads are yummy dolloped with creamy lemon mayonnaise.
To 1/2 cup mayonnaise, add 3 tablespoons each of lemon juice,
light cream and powdered sugar. Garnish with a sprinkle of
lemon zest or some carrot curls, if you like.

Grandma's Best
SIDES & SALADS

Waldorf Salad

Jean Kelly
Bruceton Mills, WV

*This recipe has been in our family for years...we serve it at
Christmas and other special occasions. For variety,
add pineapple chunks or seedless red or green grapes.*

2 c. Red Delicious apples, cored
   and chopped
1 c. celery, sliced
1/2 c. chopped walnuts
1/4 c. mayonnaise

1 T. sugar
1 t. vanilla extract
1/2 t. lemon juice
2 c. frozen whipped topping,
   thawed

In a bowl, combine apples, celery and walnuts; set aside. In a separate
large bowl, blend together mayonnaise, sugar, vanilla and lemon juice.
Fold in whipped topping; add apple mixture and stir gently. Cover and
chill until serving time. Makes 6 servings.

Grandma always had real cloth napkins on the dinner table.
Stitch fun charms to napkin rings, so everyone can identify
their own napkin easily.

Barberton Hot Rice

Linda Fleisher
New Franklin, OH

For decades, Barberton, Ohio, has claimed fame as "The Chicken Capital of the World!" My mom was a wonderful cook, but every once in awhile, as an extra-special treat, we would get chicken dinners "to go" from one of the local chicken houses. Back in the 1960s, five dollars bought two adult and four child-size dinners that consisted of delicious fried chicken, homemade fries, coleslaw and hot rice. Although each restaurant had a slightly different version of hot rice, I think my recipe captures the best in all of them. My family thinks so, too!

1/2 c. butter
2 onions, finely chopped
2 yellow hot peppers, finely
    chopped
28-oz. can whole tomatoes
15-oz. can tomato sauce

1/2 c. water
1/3 c. sugar
2-1/2 T. paprika
1/2 t. cayenne pepper
salt and pepper to taste
1/2 c. long-grain rice, uncooked

Melt butter in a large skillet over medium heat. Add onions and peppers; sauté until tender. Process undrained tomatoes in a food processor or with a hand blender. Add tomatoes to mixture in pan along with tomato sauce, water, sugar and seasonings. Bring just to a boil; reduce heat to medium-low. Cover and simmer for 30 minutes, stirring occasionally. Add uncooked rice and cook for an additional 30 minutes, or until rice is tender, stirring occasionally and adding a little more water as needed. Serves 10.

To keep rice from becoming sticky, don't stir it after cooking.
Instead, gently fluff it with a fork. It works every time!

Grandma's Sloppy Kraut

Linda Nagy
Powder Springs, GA

Growing up in a German household meant that sauerkraut was a staple and a great side dish, paired with sausage or pork and potatoes. New Year's Day was always celebrated with pork roast and Grandma's specialty...her hearty Sloppy Kraut, a German tradition for good luck throughout the year.

4 slices bacon, cut into
   1-1/2 inch pieces
14.4-oz. can sauerkraut, drained
1/2 c. onion, grated
1 small potato, grated

1 small apple, peeled, cored
   and grated
1-1/2 t. caraway seed
1/2 c. water
pepper to taste

Cook bacon in a large skillet over medium heat until almost crisp. Leave bacon and drippings in pan. Add remaining ingredients except water and pepper; stir to combine. Cook over medium heat, adding water a little at a time, until heated through. Cover and simmer over low heat for 15 minutes, stirring occasionally. Season with pepper and serve. Makes 4 to 6 servings.

Take time to share family stories and traditions with
your children. A cherished family recipe can be
a great conversation starter.

Zucchini & Squash Sauté

Sherri Tucker Fyan
Albany, NY

My grandmother and mother used to make this when I was a girl. It came about from the overabundance of vegetables from our gardens, and because there was always a crowd to feed. It pairs nicely with chicken, turkey and fish. My own twist is to add whatever suitable vegetables I have in my refrigerator. I think Grandmother and Mother would be happy that I carry on this recipe with our family gatherings.

2 T. oil
2 small zucchini, halved and
   sliced 1/2-inch thick
2 small yellow squash, halved
   and sliced 1/2-inch thick
Optional: sliced mushrooms,
   cherry tomatoes, green beans,
   onions

1 t. garlic, minced, or to taste
1 t. coarse salt
1/2 to 1 t. coarse pepper
1 to 3 t. lemon juice

In a large sauté pan with high sides, heat oil over medium to medium-high heat. Add vegetables; cook until beginning to soften, stirring slightly. Turn vegetables over; add garlic, salt and pepper. Continue to sauté until vegetables are slightly tender but not soggy, up to 15 minutes. Remove from heat; sprinkle with lemon juice. Serve immediately. Makes 6 to 8 servings.

For fresh, clean-smelling cutting boards, rub them
with the cut side of a lemon half.

Grandma's Romanian Rice Pilaf

*Patricia Nau
River Grove, IL*

*My Romanian grandmother, Emma Matison, was an
amazing cook and baker. This recipe, called Pilaf de Ciuperci
in Romanian, is one of her Lenten specials.*

2 T. butter
2 c. sliced mushrooms
12-oz. pkg. frozen chopped
    onions
2 T. fresh parsley, chopped
2 t. garlic, chopped

1 t. dried basil
1/8 t. pepper
2/3 c. long-cooking rice,
    uncooked
1-1/3 c. water

Melt butter in a saucepan over medium heat. Add mushrooms,
onions, parsley, garlic, basil and pepper. Cook, stirring often, for about
5 minutes. Stir in uncooked rice and water; bring to a boil. Reduce heat
to medium-low. Cover and simmer for about 25 minutes, until rice is
tender and liquid is absorbed. Serves 6.

An easy vinaigrette dressing for fresh salad greens...
simply whisk together 1/4 cup oil, 2 tablespoons red wine
vinegar, 2 tablespoons sugar and 1/4 teaspoon hot pepper sauce.

Mandarin Lettuce Salad

Elizabeth Smithson
Mayfield, KY

I can remember my granny making this salad for Sunday dinner and thinking, boy, we are eating like kings! She used fresh lettuce and onions grown in her own garden.

1/3 c. slivered almonds
2 T. sugar
1 bunch romaine lettuce,
   torn into bite-size pieces
1/2 head iceberg lettuce,
   torn into bite-size pieces

1 c. celery, chopped
2 green onions, chopped
11-oz. can mandarin oranges,
   drained

To caramelize almonds, add almonds and sugar to a heavy skillet over medium heat. Cook and stir until sugar melts and coats almonds. Remove from heat; set aside to cool. In a large bowl, combine remaining ingredients; toss gently. Add Dressing and toss to mix; top with almonds. Serves 8 to 10.

Dressing:

2 T. vinegar
2 T. oil
2 T. sugar

1/2 t. salt
1/8 t. pepper
1/8 t. hot pepper sauce

Combine all ingredients; whisk until sugar dissolves.

Look for distinctive dishes to use at dinnertime. Years from now, your children and grandchildren may cherish these dishes for the memories they bring back.

Scalloped Pineapple

Jennifer Hempen
Argyle, IA

*Handed down from my Great-Grandma Arlene, this recipe
is a favorite for carry-in dinners at church.*

2 20-oz. cans crushed pineapple
6 slices white bread, cubed
3/4 c. sugar
1/2 c. margarine, melted
3 eggs, beaten
1/4 c. milk
1/8 t. salt
1/8 t. nutmeg

In a large bowl, combine pineapple with juice and remaining ingredients
except nutmeg. Mix well; transfer to an 11"x9" baking pan. Sprinkle
with nutmeg. Bake, uncovered, at 350 degrees for 40 minutes, or until
golden. Makes 8 to 10 servings.

Pickled Peaches

Judy Phelan
Macomb, IL

*This is a recipe from my maternal grandmother, which she
always made for the winter holidays. These are especially
good served with baked ham.*

3 29-oz. cans yellow cling
   peach halves
3/4 c. brown sugar, packed
1/2 c. vinegar
2 4-inch cinnamon sticks
1 t. whole cloves
1 t. whole allspice

Drain peaches, reserving the juice from one can. Place peaches in a
bowl and set aside. In a saucepan, combine reserved peach juice, sugar,
vinegar and spices. Bring to a boil over medium heat; boil for 5 minutes.
Pour over peaches; allow peaches to cool. Cover and refrigerate for
10 to 14 days before serving. Makes 2 quarts.

For tasty, bright-colored vegetables, add a tablespoon or 2
of vinegar to the water when boiling or steaming.

Grandma's Eggplant Casserole

Katie Wollgast
Troy, MO

My grandma always made this dish when Grandpa brought in fresh eggplant and tomatoes from the garden. It tastes something like pizza. I like to serve it as a side dish with Italian mains, or as a meatless main dish...may want to double it for that!

1 eggplant, peeled and cubed	1/2 c. saltine cracker crumbs
1 c. onion, chopped	1/4 lb. pasteurized process
1-1/2 t. salt, divided	cheese, very thinly sliced
1/4 t. pepper	2 ripe tomatoes, thinly sliced
1/2 t. garlic powder	1/4 c. grated Parmesan cheese
1 t. dried oregano	dried parsley to taste
2 eggs, beaten	

In a large saucepan, combine eggplant, onion and one teaspoon salt; add water just to cover. Bring to a boil over medium heat. Cook until eggplant is just tender, but not soft. Drain well; cool slightly. Add remaining salt, pepper, garlic powder, oregano, eggs and cracker crumbs; stir gently to combine. Transfer half of mixture to a greased 2-quart casserole dish; arrange cheese slices over top. Cover with remaining eggplant mixture. Arrange tomato slices over top in a pretty pattern. Sprinkle with grated cheese and parsley. Bake, uncovered, at 375 degrees for 30 minutes,or until hot and lightly golden. Makes 4 to 6 servings.

Hang a small blackboard in the kitchen and update it daily with chalk...everyone is sure to hurry to the dinner table when they know what's for dinner!

Grandma's Best
SIDES & SALADS

Gram's Haluski

Ange Sukala
Williamsburg, PA

My Gram and Ma made this when I was growing up,
and it's still my all-time favorite comfort food.

16-oz. pkg. medium-wide egg
  noodles, uncooked
1 c. butter

2 small heads cabbage, cored and
  cut into 1-inch pieces
salt and pepper to taste

Cook noodles according to package directions, until tender but still
slightly firm. Drain noodles well and set aside. In the same pot, melt
butter over medium-low heat. Add cabbage and cook until soft but not
browned. Season with salt and pepper. Mix in cooked noodles and heat
until warmed through. Makes 8 servings.

Fried Green Beans

Elizabeth Smithson
Mayfield, KY

This is the only way my kids and grands will eat their veggies! It's
always a hit at family gatherings and church dinners. If you want to
use fresh green beans, cook them until nearly tender before adding to
the skillet.

1/2 c. butter
1/2 c. onion, chopped
1/3 c. brown sugar, packed

2/3 c. real bacon bits
4 14-1/2 oz. cans cut
  green beans

Add butter and onion to a skillet. Cook over medium heat for 5 minutes.
Add brown sugar, bacon bits and beans with juice. Cook over low heat
until liquid is mostly evaporated, stirring often. Serves 10 to 12.

Cook egg noodles the easy way...no watching needed. Bring water
to a rolling boil, then turn off the heat. Add noodles. Cover and
let stand for 20 minutes, stirring once or twice.

Grandma's Best
COMFORT FOODS

Grandma Betty's Jalapeño Cornbread Casserole

Theresa Eldridge
Festus, MO

My grandma was such a sweetheart. She was with us until the age of 102! She was such a spunky little lady and this was one of her yummiest dishes...it's easy too. Enjoy!

15-1/4 oz. can corn, drained and
    very well rinsed
14-3/4 oz. can cream-style corn
4-oz. can chopped green chiles or
    jalapeños, well drained
8-oz. pkg. corn muffin mix

8-oz. container sour cream
1/4 c. butter, melted
2 T. sugar or honey
1 c. finely shredded mild Cheddar
    or Colby Jack cheese

In a large bowl, combine all ingredients except shredded cheese; mix well. Spread batter evenly in a greased 13"x9" baking pan; top with cheese. Cover and bake at 350 degrees for 50 minutes. Uncover and bake for an additional 10 to 15 minutes, until beginning to turn golden. Remove from oven; let stand for 5 minutes and cut into squares. Serves 6 to 8.

Grandma's vintage kitchen utensils make a nostalgic display
for your kitchen when arranged on a grapevine wreath
with raffia ties.

Grandma's Best
SIDES & SALADS

Tomato Fritters

Deanne Corona
Hampton, GA

I have no idea where my grandmother picked up this gem of a recipe...
she was using it as a bookmark in one of her cookbooks. The first time
I tried it, I fell in love. It's really good with chicken or any other main
dish. I love tomatoes and can eat them off the vine just as they are,
but sometimes they just need that extra oomph. So here is one of my
favorite sides using fresh tomatoes!

1 c. all-purpose flour
1 t. baking powder
1 t. fresh rosemary, snipped
1/8 t. salt
1/8 t. pepper
1 c. ripe tomatoes, cut into
    1/2-inch cubes

2 T. onion or leek, finely chopped
1 T. fresh basil, snipped
1/8 t. Worcestershire sauce
1 egg, beaten
oil for frying
Optional: cheese or jalapeño jelly

In a bowl, combine flour, baking powder, rosemary, salt and pepper. Pat tomatoes dry; add to flour mixture. Add remaining ingredients except egg, oil and optional ingredients; don't mix yet. Add egg and stir everything together. In a large skillet over medium-high heat, heat several inches oil to at least 360 degrees. Drop batter into oil by tablespoonfuls, lightly patting them down a bit into the hot oil. Cook until golden on both sides; drain on paper towels. Serve with cheese or jalapeño jelly, if desired. Serves 4 to 6.

For good old-fashioned fun, take the kids to a nearby pick-your-own peach orchard or strawberry farm. Give them each a bucket and pretend not to notice when they nibble on their pickings!

Texas Shrimp Salad

Sue Morrison
Blue Springs, MO

This was my mother's recipe from southeast Texas. Its unique blend of potatoes, peas and shrimp makes a tasty dish. I grew up in Beaumont, Texas, but have lived in Missouri for over 50 years. Mother would make this salad on a hot summer day. We'd fill our plates and go outdoors to eat under a huge oak tree. The cool shade was wonderful... there was no air conditioning at that time. Eating outdoors was a real treat. There was always lemonade or iced tea, too!

2 baking potatoes, cooked,
    peeled and cubed
2 eggs, hard-boiled, peeled
    and chopped
6-oz. can salad shrimp, drained

1/4 c. green onions, chopped
1/4 c. celery, chopped
1 T. lemon juice
1 c. baby peas, drained
salt and pepper to taste

Combine all ingredients in a large bowl. Pour Dressing over all; toss lightly to coat well. Cover and chill until serving time. Makes 4 to 6 servings.

Dressing:

1/2 c. mayonnaise-style
    salad dressing
1 T. mustard

1 t. vinegar
1/2 t. sugar
salt and pepper to taste

Blend together all ingredients.

Taking a salad to a family get-together? Mix it up in a plastic zipping bag instead of a bowl, seal and set it on ice in a picnic cooler. No more worries about leaks or spills!

Old-Fashioned Overnight Slaw

Joan Chance
Houston, TX

*This recipe was from my mom and I'm more than 80 years old...
so you know I have liked it for quite awhile!*

1 head cabbage, thinly sliced
3/4 c. onion, thinly sliced
1/2 c. green pepper, sliced
   into rings
1 c. sugar

1 c. vinegar
1 t. celery seed
salt to taste
1/2 c. oil

Combine cabbage, onion and pepper rings in a bowl; set aside. In a saucepan, combine sugar, vinegar, celery seed and salt. Bring to a boil over medium heat, stirring until sugar dissolves. Gradually add oil to hot mixture. Pour over cabbage mixture while hot. Cover and refrigerate overnight before serving. Makes 8 to 10 servings.

Host a recipe swap. Invite friends to bring a favorite casserole along
with enough recipe cards for each guest. While everyone enjoys
a delicious potluck, collect the recipe cards, staple together
and hand out when it's time to depart.

Mom's Dirty Rice

Betty Kozlowski
Newnan, GA

We had a large family, and all of us loved Mom's Dirty Rice! Whenever we visited Grandma's for a butchering, this Cajun-style rice dressing was always on the menu, along with cracklings made using the fresh pork.

1 lb. chicken livers	5 c. water, divided
1 lb. chicken gizzards	2 to 3 t. salt
1 T. oil	2 c. long-grain rice, uncooked
1 T. butter	1 t. pepper
1 lb. ground pork	Garnish: chopped green onion,
2 onions, chopped	fresh parsley
1 green pepper, chopped	

In a food processor, grind chicken livers and gizzards; set aside. Add livers, gizzards and oil to a large skillet over medium heat; cook until browned. Drain, leaving livers and gizzards in pan. To the same pan, add butter, pork, onions and green pepper. Sauté for 5 minutes. Add one cup water; cover and simmer for 5 minutes. Uncover and cook until liquid is absorbed. Add salt and remaining water. Bring to a boil over high heat. Stir in uncooked rice and pepper; bring to a boil again. Reduce heat to medium-low; cover and simmer for 15 minutes. Gently fold rice mixture from top to bottom with a large spoon. Cover and cook for about 5 to 10 minutes, until rice is tender and water is absorbed. Garnish as desired and serve. Makes 8 servings.

Hosting a family get-together? Ask each family member to bring a baby photo. Post them all on a big board... first person to guess who's who gets a prize!

Grandma's Best
SIDES & SALADS

Cheesy Potatoes

Cathy Neeley
North Logan, UT

This family recipe comes down from my grandmother. Her mother died when she was a baby and she was passed from family to family while she was growing up. Her older sister, my Great-Aunt Olive, said this recipe was a family favorite that my great-grandmother had made. We have simplified it using frozen hashbrowns, but it can be made with boiled, cooled shredded potatoes as well. We make this at every family gathering, including camp-outs made in a Dutch oven, foil pans at Lake Powell and in our smoker in the backyard. It never disappoints... it's simple cheesy goodness that everyone loves. Enjoy this like crazy, we do!

2 32-oz. pkgs. frozen shredded
   hashbrowns, thawed
2 8-oz. pkgs. shredded medium
   or sharp Cheddar cheese

salt and pepper to taste
1 pt. whipping cream

Spray a 13"x9" baking pan with non-stick vegetable spray. Layer one package hashbrowns and one package shredded cheese; season with salt and pepper. Repeat layering; drizzle with cream. Cover with aluminum foil. Bake at 350 degrees for 35 to 45 minutes, until bubbly in the center and cheese is melted. Makes 9 to 12 servings.

Bring out Grandma's cheery fruit or flower table linens
for special family get-togethers...sure to inspire conversations
about other special gatherings.

Lillian's 7-Layer Salad

Debbie Dowen
Schodack Landing, NY

I first tasted this delicious salad at my Grandmother's 90th birthday party. It was a glorious summer day in June and we had a big picnic on my aunt & uncle's front lawn. Everybody brought something...this salad was so delicious that I asked around to find out who made it so I could get the recipe! Fortunately, I didn't have to ask too many people, because my Aunt Lillian was the one who made it. We have been enjoying it every since. Friends request that I bring it whenever we are invited to picnics and dinners. So delicious!

1 head iceberg lettuce, chopped
    into 1-inch pieces
1 c. celery, sliced
1-1/2 c. red onions, sliced
1 c. frozen peas
1 lb. bacon, crisply cooked and
    crumbled

1-1/2 c. shredded sharp Cheddar
    cheese
2 T. sugar
1-1/2 c. mayonnaise

In a tall, narrow bowl, evenly layer lettuce, celery, onions, peas, bacon and cheese in the order listed. Set aside. In a small bowl, whisk sugar into mayonnaise until consistency changes slightly. Spread over salad, covering completely and spreading to the edges. Cover with plastic wrap and refrigerate overnight. About 30 minutes before serving, toss salad and mix well. It's easiest to transfer the salad into a huge bowl for mixing, and then back into a serving bowl. Serves 12.

Ask family & friends to share copies of tried & true
recipe favorites and create a special cookbook...a great gift
for a new cook in the family.

Grandma's Best
SIDES & SALADS

Grandma's Party Salad

Julie Preston
Edwardsville, IL

For every family get-together, Grandma would make her yummy vegetable salad. We all loved it and would beg for more!

1 bunch broccoli, chopped	3/4 c. sugar
1 head cauliflower, chopped	3 T. white vinegar
1 red onion, diced	8-oz. can cashews
1-1/2 c. mayonnaise	

Combine vegetables in a large bowl; set aside. In a separate bowl, mix together mayonnaise, sugar and vinegar. Pour over vegetables; toss to mix well. Cover and chill for 30 minutes. Just before serving, add cashews and toss again. Makes 10 servings.

"Adopt" an older neighbor as a grandparent. Include them in the children's ball games and family outings...bake cookies together and share stories over dinner. Your family can help out by running errands, weeding flower beds and raking leaves...it's sure to be rewarding for everybody.

Carrots Buffet

Jennifer Lyda
Greenwood, SC

Grandma used to make this delicious dish for church potlucks and around the holidays to serve with her Swedish meatballs.

12 carrots, peeled and sliced
1/2 c. onion, diced or grated
1 c. plus 1 T. butter, divided
1/4 c. all-purpose flour
1/4 t. dry mustard
1/4 t. celery salt

1 t. salt
1/8 t. pepper
2 c. milk
8-oz. pkg. shredded sharp
    Cheddar cheese
2 c. soft bread crumbs

Fill a large saucepan with water; bring to a boil over medium-high heat. Add carrots and boil for 10 minutes; drain. Meanwhile, in a skillet over medium heat, sauté onion in one cup butter until tender. Add flour, seasonings and milk; cook and stir until thickened. In a buttered 2-quart casserole dish, layer half of carrots and half of shredded cheese. Repeat layering, ending with cheese. Pour sauce over all. Melt remaining butter and toss with bread crumbs; sprinkle over casserole. Bake, uncovered, at 350 degrees for 25 minutes, or until bubbly and golden. Makes 8 servings.

Use a damp sponge sprinkled with baking soda to scrub fruits & veggies...it works just as well as expensive cleansers for vegetables.

Gram's Savory Potato Cakes

Sandy Coffey
Cincinnati, OH

My grandma used to make these potato cakes on special Sundays,
and I have done the same for my kids and grandkids.

2 c. potatoes, peeled, quartered
    and cooked
1 egg, separated
2 T. butter, melted and slightly
    cooled

1/2 t. salt
1/4 t. paprika
2 T. water
2 T. dry bread crumbs
1 to 2 T. oil or butter

Press hot potatoes through a ricer or food mill; set aside. In a bowl,
whisk together egg yolk, melted butter and seasonings. Add to potatoes;
mix well and shape into flattened cakes. In a small bowl, beat egg white
and water. Dip potato cakes into egg white; roll in bread crumbs. Heat
oil or butter in a skillet over medium heat; add potato cakes. Cook until
golden on both sides. Serves 4 to 6.

Wilted Lettuce Salad

Judy Scherer
Benton, MO

My mother would fix this tasty old-fashioned salad with fresh lettuce,
onions and radishes that she'd picked from her garden.

4 to 5 c. romaine lettuce or other
    favorite lettuce, torn
Optional: sliced radishes and
    onions to taste
2 to 3 slices bacon

1/4 c. oil
1/4 c. vinegar
2 to 3 t. sugar
salt and pepper to taste

In a bowl, combine lettuce, radishes and onions, if using; set aside. In
a skillet over medium heat, cook bacon until crisp. Remove bacon to
a paper towel; reserve drippings in skillet. Add oil and vinegar to
drippings; heat until hot. Add sugar; stir until dissolved. Pour hot
mixture over lettuce mixture and toss to mix well. Season with salt
and pepper; top with crumbled bacon and serve immediately. Makes
5 servings.

Grandma's Best
COMFORT FOODS

Iris's Apple Noodle Kugel

Patricia Nau
River Grove, IL

Iris was a very good friend of our family. During the holidays, she would make this delicious pudding and deliver it to my grandmother's house. She gave this recipe to my mother in the 1950s. Recently I came across it in an old cookbook and made it myself...delicious!

16-oz. pkg. egg noodles,
   uncooked
1/2 c. golden raisins
1 c. hot water
4 eggs
3/4 c. sugar

2 t. cinnamon
1/2 c. butter, melted
1/2 t. vanilla extract
1/2 t. lemon juice
4 apples, peeled, cored and
   thinly sliced

Cook noodles according to package directions; drain. Meanwhile, cover raisins with hot water; let stand for 5 minutes and drain. In a large bowl, beat eggs well. Add sugar, cinnamon, melted butter, vanilla, lemon juice, apples and raisins; stir well. Add cooked noodles, stirring until well combined. Spread mixture in a lightly greased 13"x9" baking pan. Bake, uncovered, at 350 degrees for 45 to 60 minutes, until bubbly and golden. Makes 8 servings.

Enjoy seasonal fruits & veggies...strawberries and asparagus in spring, corn and tomatoes in summer, acorn squash and pears in fall, cabbage and apples in winter. You'll be serving your family the tastiest, healthiest produce year 'round.

Mabel's Sweet Potato Puffs

Judy MacInnes
San Diego, CA

This recipe was handed down by my grandmother, Mabel Cheever, to my mom, Marge. We had them every Thanksgiving and Christmas...a family tradition! They're delicious.

2 c. sweet potatoes, peeled
  and cooked
1 egg, beaten
2 T. butter, softened

1/2 t. salt
7 to 8 large marshmallows
2 c. crispy rice cereal, crushed
1/4 c. butter, melted

In a bowl, mash sweet potatoes. Add egg, softened butter and salt. Pat some of mixture around each marshmallow. In another bowl, combine crushed cereal and melted butter. Roll puffs in cereal mixture; arrange in a buttered 13"x9" baking pan. Bake, uncovered, at 350 degrees for about one hour. Makes 7 to 8 puffs.

Carrie's Mashed Sweet Potato Caramel

Sandy Coffey
Cincinnati, OH

This dish is great with meatloaf! For Sunday dinner after church at Grandma Carrie's, there was always something yummy cooking. I have fond childhood memories of her and continue with her recipes to this day. Leftover sweet potatoes can be used.

2 c. sweet potatoes, peeled
  and cooked
1/4 to 1/2 c. half-and-half
  or milk

salt and pepper to taste
1/2 c. thick maple syrup
1/4 c. butter, melted

Mash potatoes in a bowl, adding enough half-and-half or milk to make a smooth soft paste. Season with salt and pepper. Spread in a well-greased 8"x8" baking pan. Drizzle with maple syrup and melted butter. Bake, uncovered, at 400 degrees for 15 minutes, or until golden and caramelized on top. Serves 3to 4.

Grandma's Best
COMFORT FOODS

Grandma's German Potato Salad

Vivian Marshall
Columbus, OH

This recipe is my grandma's recipe from our family cookbook and it is close to a hundred years old. No changes have been made to it. We live by the rule, "if it's not broke...don't fix it!" It's a great side for sausage or ham. So good!

4 to 5 potatoes, cubed
4 slices bacon
1/2 c. onion, chopped, or 4 green
  onions, sliced
1 T. all-purpose flour
1/3 c. cider vinegar
1 T. sugar
1 t. dry mustard
1 t. salt
1/2 c. water
3 to 4 eggs, hard-boiled,
  peeled and chopped

In a large saucepan, cover unpeeled, cubed potatoes with water. Boil over medium-high heat just until fork-tender, but not too soft. Drain and set aside in a large bowl. Meanwhile, in a skillet over medium heat, cook bacon until crisp. Set bacon aside to drain, reserving drippings in skillet. Add onion to reserved drippings; cook until softened. Add flour, vinegar, sugar, seasonings and water to skillet; cook and stir until smooth and thick. Pour hot mixture over potatoes; toss to coat. Serve warm, garnished with crumbled bacon and chopped eggs. Makes 5 to 6 servings.

It takes a heap o' livin' in a house to make it home.
–Edgar A. Guest

Broccoli-Rice Casserole

Linda Machado
Melba, ID

My sister-in-law used to fix this dish for family gatherings when I first got married in 1971. I liked it so well, I finally got the recipe from her a year later. I think about her every time I fix it. When I take it to potlucks, I always have requests for the recipe and an empty dish to bring home! I've made this recipe for over 45 years and it never gets old.

7-oz. pkg. fried rice-flavored
    rice vermicelli mix
10-oz. pkg. frozen broccoli cuts
    or spears
8-oz. container sour cream, room
    temperature

4-oz. can diced green chiles
8-oz. pkg. shredded mozzarella
    cheese

Cook rice mix according to package directions; set aside. Separately cook broccoli according to package directions; drain. Spread rice mix in a 13"x9" baking pan lightly coated with non-stick vegetable spray. Evenly layer sour cream, chiles, broccoli and shredded cheese over rice. Bake, uncovered, at 375 degrees for 35 to 45 minutes, just until bubbly and cheese just starts to turn golden at the edges. Makes 6 to 8 servings.

Grandma knew this little trick for softening unripe fruit...
simply place it in a brown paper bag on the countertop.
It'll ripen in no time at all.

Grandma's Best
COMFORT FOODS

Corn Fritters

Tina Goodpasture
Meadowview, VA

I was raised in the south and we had cornbread at every meal. I can still see my Granny Hudson's table, always loaded with good food... beans, homemade cornbread, apple butter, green beans and lots more. Those were the days! These fritters are a favorite.

1/2 c. all-purpose flour
1 t. baking powder
1 t. salt
1 t. butter, melted

2 eggs, beaten
1/2 c. milk
11-oz. can corn, drained
shortening or oil for frying

In a bowl, sift together flour, baking powder and salt. Add butter, eggs, milk and corn; beat well. Heat one inch of shortening or oil in a skillet over medium-high heat. Drop batter by tablespoonfuls into shortening; cook until golden. Drain on paper towels. Makes 4 to 6 servings.

Grandma probably used lard for most of her frying.
Nowadays, unless a recipe specifies otherwise, canola oil is
a good choice for frying. It can stand up to high heat
without smoking or burning.

Grandma's Best
SIDES & SALADS

Bacon-Pea Salad

Irene Robinson
Cincinnati, OH

A great old-fashioned salad to take to a gathering. The recipe can easily be doubled. Add more bacon, if you like!

16-oz. pkg. frozen peas, thawed
1/3 c. red onion, chopped
1/2 c. shredded sharp Cheddar
    cheese
1/2 c. ranch salad dressing

1/4 t. salt
1/4 t. pepper
4 slices bacon, crisply cooked
    and crumbled

Combine all ingredients except bacon in a large bowl; mix gently. Cover and refrigerate for 30 minutes. Add bacon just before serving. Makes 6 servings.

Granny's Cucumber Salad

Karen Crosby
Summerville, SC

This is a recipe handed down from my grandmother, who always fixed it for Sunday dinner. It is a favorite of all my family. Her recipe also calls for diced onions, but since I don't like onions, I leave them out.

3 T. plus 2 t. mayonnaise
3 T. white vinegar
2 T. oil
salt to taste

Optional: diced onion to taste
1 to 2 cucumbers, peeled and
    sliced in very thin rounds

In a bowl, whisk together all ingredients, folding in cucumbers last. Sauce should be tangy and liquidy; add a litle more mayonnaise or vinegar, if desired. Cover and rrefrigerate before serving, if desired. Makes 4 servings.

Don't cry! Freeze onions for 5 minutes before
slicing or chopping them.

Grandma's Best
COMFORT FOODS

Watergate Salad

Judy Scherer
Benton, MO

My grandmother made this refreshing salad for all of our holiday meals.

8-oz. container frozen whipped topping, thawed
3-oz. pkg. instant pistachio pudding mix
20-oz. can pineapple chunks
1 c. mini marshmallows
1/2 c. chopped pecans or walnuts

Spoon whipped topping into a bowl; fold in dry pudding mix. Add pineapple with juice, marshmallows and nuts. Cover and refrigerate until serving time. Makes 10 servings.

Cinnamon Apples

Joan Chance
Houston, TX

A tried & true recipe from a dear old friend from long, long ago when we both lived in Washington state.

2 c. sugar
1/2 c. boiling water
1/4 c. red cinnamon candies
Optional: few drops red food coloring
1 t. vinegar
4 to 5 apples, peeled, cored and sliced
ruffled lettuce leaves

In a saucepan, combine all ingredients except apples and lettuce. Bring to a boil over medium heat; simmer and stir for 5 minutes. Add apple slices to syrup, a few at a time; cook until soft. Transfer apples to a jar; cover with the syrup and refrigerate until needed. To serve, place apple slices on a lettuce leaf. Makes 8 to 10 servings.

Serve a fruit salad in orange cups... so pretty on a dinner table! Simply cut large oranges in half and scoop out the orange pulp with a grapefruit spoon.

COMFORT FOOD
Dinner Classics

Grandma's Best
COMFORT FOODS

Grandma's Diner Steaks

Caroline Timbs
Cord, AR

I loved Granny's chicken-fried steaks and gravy. In her younger days, she worked at an old-time diner, where she learned to master the recipe. She always served them with another one of my favorites, fresh field peas with fresh snap beans in them. Best dinner around!

3 c. all-purpose flour
1 t. salt
2 t. pepper
3 eggs, beaten
2 c. Bulgarian-style buttermilk

8 beef cube steaks
oil for frying
12-oz. can evaporated milk
1 to 1-1/2 c. milk
salt and pepper to taste

Mix flour, salt and pepper in a shallow dish; whisk together eggs and buttermilk in another dish. Dip steaks into flour mixture, then into egg mixture, then into flour again. Reserve remaining flour mixture. Heat 1/2 inch oil in a skillet over medium heat. Cook steaks on each side until golden; do not overcook. Set aside steaks on a plate, reserving 3 tablespoons drippings in pan. Add 4 tablespoons reserved flour mixture; cook and stir over medium heat with a whisk until golden. Stir in milks; cook and whisk until thickened. Season with salt and pepper; serve gravy over steaks. Makes 8 servings.

A trusty cast-iron skillet was Grandma's secret to magic in the kitchen. Watch for old skillets at yard sales...often they just need a light scrub. Re-season by brushing lightly with oil and baking at 350 degrees for one hour. Turn off oven; let skillet cool in the oven before using.

COMFORT FOOD
Dinner Classics

Mock Chicken Legs

Janis Swoboda
Kennewick, WA

This recipe is from my great-grandparents, who were from England. My grandmother passed it on to my mother. Serve with gravy and mashed potatoes or steamed rice...yummy!

2 boneless, skinless chicken
   breasts
4 to 5 boneless pork chops
1 lb. beef top round steak
2 eggs, beaten
1 c. milk

1 t. dried rosemary
1 t. dried fennel
salt and pepper to taste
1 sleeve saltine crackers,
   very finely crushed
oil for frying

Tenderize all meats with a tenderizing mallet; cut into 1-1/2 inch cubes. Thread cubes onto 6-inch wood or bamboo skewers, alternating meats and leaving 1/2-inch empty on ends. Set aside. Whisk together eggs, milk and seasonings in a bowl. Place cracker crumbs in another bowl. Dip "chicken legs" (skewers) into egg mixture; carefully pat on crushed crackers. Heat one inch oil in a large skillet over medium heat. Add skewers, a few at a time. Partially cover skillet; cook and turn until crisp and golden. Makes 4 servings, about 4 pieces each.

A fresh green salad goes well with all kinds of main dishes.
For a zippy lemon dressing, shake up 1/2 cup olive oil, 1/3 cup fresh
lemon juice and one tablespoon of Dijon mustard in
a small jar. Chill to blend.

Grandma's Best
COMFORT FOODS

Pork Chops & Rice

Jenny Granovsky
Saint Paul, MN

This is a delicious recipe that my mother-in-law used to make for her family. I never got to meet her, as she died when my husband was young, but I make this recipe in memory of her. It's a quick & easy meal to make ahead of time for busy families.

4 to 6 bone-in pork chops
10-3/4 oz. can tomato soup
1/4 c. brown sugar, packed
1/4 c. vinegar
1 t. chili powder

1 t. celery seed
2 t. salt
Optional: 1/2 t. paprika
cooked rice

Arrange pork chops in a lightly greased 13"x9" baking pan; set aside. In a bowl, combine remaining ingredients except rice; spoon over chops. Cover with aluminum foil. Bake at 325 degrees for 1-1/2 hours. Uncover; spoon sauce in pan over chops and return to oven for 30 minutes more. Serve with cooked rice. Serves 4 to 6.

Railroad Cornbread

Carolyn Russell
Clyde, NC

When I first married my husband, everyone got together for a family meal and his Aunt Nettie made her Railroad Cornbread. With its cornbread topping, this quickly became one of my favorite dishes. Every time I saw his Aunt Nettie, I would ask her for Railroad Cornbread.

2 10-oz. pkgs. frozen mixed
  vegetables, thawed
2 6-oz. cans chicken, flaked
10-3/4 oz. can cream of
  chicken soup

10-3/4 oz. can cream of
  mushroom soup
8-oz. pkg. corn muffin mix

In a large bowl, combine all ingredients except corn muffin mix. Transfer to a greased 12"x9" glass baking pan; set aside. Prepare muffin mix according to package directions; pour batter over vegetable mixture. Bake, uncovered, at 375 degrees for 15 to 20 minutes, until heated through and cornbread is done. Cut into squares. Makes 6 to 8 servings.

Dad's Hamburger Steaks in Mushroom Gravy

Pam Lunn
Pensacola, FL

My father made these delicious hamburger steaks with gravy for years. He is now in his 80s and no longer cooks, so now I make them for him. These are good served with mashed potatoes, buttered corn and hot rolls.

1-1/2 lbs. ground beef
1 egg, beaten
1/2 to 3/4 c. Italian-seasoned
   dry bread crumbs
1-1/2 T. onion powder

1-1/2 t. seasoned salt
1/4 t. pepper
4 T. catsup, divided
2 10-3/4 oz. cans golden
   mushroom soup

In a large bowl, combine beef, egg, bread crumbs, seasonings and 3 tablespoons catsup. Stir to thoroughly combine. Shape beef mixture into 6 oval patties. Add patties to a large cast-iron skillet. Cook over medium heat until browned on one side; turn patties over and continue to brown. In a bowl, combine mushroom soup and remaining catsup; stir to blend. Drain pan; spoon soup mixture over patties. Reduce heat to low. Cover and cook for 20 to 25 minutes, checking often to make sure patties don't burn on the bottom. Serve patties topped with gravy from skillet. Serves 6.

Invite the new neighbors to share a meal...it's what Grandma would do. Send them home with a gift basket filled with flyers from favorite bakeries and pizza parlors, coupons and local maps...tuck in a package of homemade cookies. What a friendly gesture!

Grandma's Best
COMFORT FOODS

Chicken & Vegetable Pot Pie

Jane Granger
Manteno, IL

This is always a favorite meal of my daughter, husband and granddaughters. It's simple to make.

1 T. butter
10-3/4 oz. can cream of
   chicken soup
10-3/4 oz. can cream of
   mushroom soup
1/2 c. milk
1/2 t. onion powder

1/4 t. dried thyme
1/8 t. pepper
2 c. frozen mixed vegetables,
   thawed
4 c. cooked chicken, cubed
10-oz. tube refrigerated flaky
   biscuits, quartered

Melt butter in a large skillet over medium heat; stir in soups, milk and seasonings until smooth. Add vegetables and chicken; mix well and heat through. Spoon mixture into a greased 12"x8" glass baking pan. Arrange biscuit pieces over hot mixture. Bake, uncovered, at 375 degrees for 20 to 25 minutes, until filling is bubbly and biscuits are golden. Serves 6.

For the juiciest, most flavorful chicken, cover it with water and simmer gently just until tender. Then turn off the heat and let the chicken cool in its own broth.

COMFORT FOOD
Dinner Classics

Grandma's Macaroni & Cheese
Patricia Nau
River Grove, IL

My grandmother used to make this on Fridays during Lent, and it was always delicious. My family loves this dish, any day of the week! Brick cheese from Wisconsin is what gives this dish its creaminess, but if you can't find it, Cheddar cheese works well.

16-oz. pkg. elbow macaroni,
   uncooked
16-oz. pkg. pasteurized process
   cheese, cubed
1-1/2 c. milk, divided
1/4 c. butter, sliced

2 eggs, lightly beaten
4 c. brick cheese, shredded
   and divided
1 t. kosher salt
pepper to taste

Cook macaroni according to package directions. Drain well and transfer to a large bowl. Meanwhile, in a saucepan over low heat, melt process cheese with 3/4 cup milk, stirring often. Pour melted cheese sauce over macaroni; stir. Add butter, eggs, remaining milk, one cup brick cheese, salt and pepper; mix well. Transfer mixture to a greased 2-quart casserole dish. Sprinkle remaining brick cheese on top. Bake, uncovered, at 375 degrees for about 30 minutes, until bubbly and golden. Makes 6 to 8 servings.

It's a lovely thing...everyone sitting down together,
sharing food.
–Alice May Brock

Grandma's Best
COMFORT FOODS

River House Casserole

Macey Smith
Winter Haven, FL

My sweet Grandma Judy used to make this hamburger casserole all the time for my sister and me at her river house. I loved it so much, I had her write it down for me so my mom could make it. Now I make it for my family. It is the ultimate comfort dish, and even pleases picky toddlers. Grandma is the true definition of a Southern cook...I am so grateful for her and all the things she has taught me in the kitchen. If I'm not quite sure what I'm doing with a recipe, she is always a phone call away and to the rescue. Her favorite advice...measure with your heart.

1-1/2 lbs. ground beef
1 onion, diced
8-oz. elbow macaroni, uncooked
28-oz. can stewed tomatoes
8-oz. can tomato sauce

8-oz. pkg. cream cheese,
    room temperature, cubed
8-oz. container sour cream
8-oz. pkg. shredded Cheddar
    cheese

In a large skillet over medium heat, brown beef with onion; drain and set aside. In a large saucepan, combine uncooked macaroni, stewed tomatoes with juice and tomato sauce; add some water if needed to cover ingredients. Cook over medium heat, stirring occasionally, until macaroni is nearly tender. Mix in beef mixture. Add cream cheese and sour cream; stir until everything is mixed well and melted together. Transfer to a greased 3-quart large casserole dish. Top with shredded cheese. Bake, uncovered, at 325 degrees for 20 minutes. Makes 6 to 8 servings.

Celebrate Grandparents' Day, September 12, by inviting Grandma & Grandpa to Sunday dinner. Let them take it easy while the rest of the family does all the cooking and serving!

COMFORT FOOD
Dinner Classics

Stir-Fry Chicken

Kayla Camp
Kilgore, TX

My great-grandmother used to make this yummy chicken dish all the time. Whenever I make it, I think of her and her sweet smile!

2 T. soy sauce
1 T. cornstarch
2 cloves garlic, minced
Optional: 2 T. dry sherry
2 boneless, skinless chicken
   breasts, thinly sliced

2 T. oil
1/2 lb. broccoli, chopped
1/2 c. onion, thinly sliced
1 carrot, peeled and thinly sliced
cooked rice

In a small bowl, combine soy sauce, cornstarch, garlic and sherry, if using; mix well and set aside. In a wok or large skillet over medium heat, sauté chicken in oil for 2 minutes. Add vegetables; cook and stir for 3 more minutes, or until tender. Add soy sauce mixture; cook and stir until slightly thickened. To serve, ladle over hot cooked rice. Makes 6 servings.

Serve up a seasoned rice dish..no boxed mix needed. Sauté 1/4 cup each chopped onion and celery in a little oil until tender. Add 2 cups water and bring to a boil. Stir in one cup long-cooking rice and 2 chicken bouillon cubes. Reduce heat to medium-low. Cover and simmer for 20 to 25 minutes, until rice is tender.

Bundle Burgers

Anne Hansen
Fort Myers, FL

My mother-in-law first made this dish and we all fell in love with it. So easy and tasty, it readily became our favorite family dinner. The hamburger is pressed thin, so it cooks easily. Whenever I have made it for company, they ask me for the recipe. Serve with mashed potatoes, topping with pan gravy. Yum!

6-oz. pkg. chicken-flavored
    stuffing mix
2 lbs. ground beef
salt and pepper to taste
2 10-3/4 oz. cans golden
    mushroom soup

5-oz. can evaporated milk
3 T. catsup
1 T. Worcestershire sauce
Optional: 4-oz. can sliced
    mushrooms, drained

Prepare stuffing according to package directions; set aside to cool slightly. Form beef into 6 balls. Working with one ball at a time, place a ball between 2 pieces of wax paper. Press flat, using the heel of your hand. Season patty with salt and pepper. Spoon 2 to 3 tablespoons stuffing into the center of patty. Using your hands on the outside of the bottom wax paper, draw the patty up and press the top together (this forms the bundle). Place in a greased 13"x9" baking pan. In a bowl, whisk together remaining ingredients, adding any leftover dressing, if you like. Spoon over bundles. Bake, uncovered, at 350 degrees for 35 to 45 minutes, until bundles are cooked through and gravy is bubbly. Serves 4 to 6.

Mashed potatoes are the perfect partner for creamy comfort foods, and they're ready in a jiffy. Quarter potatoes (no peeling required!) and cook in boiling water until tender, 10 to 20 minutes. Drain, mash right in the pan and stir in butter and a little milk to desired consistency.

COMFORT FOOD
Dinner Classics

Tamale Pie

Mary Oerline
Ann Arbor, MI

A favorite recipe from my husband's grandmother.

8-oz. pkg. corn muffin mix
1 lb. ground beef
3/4 c. onion, chopped
1 green pepper, chopped

1 c. mild or medium salsa
1 c. shredded Cheddar cheese
Garnish: salsa, sour cream

Prepare corn muffin mix according to package instructions. Spread a thin layer of batter in the bottom of a greased 8"x8" baking pan; set aside. In a skillet over medium heat, brown beef with onion and green pepper. Drain; stir in salsa. Spread beef mixture over batter in pan; top with remaining batter. Bake, uncovered, at 350 degrees for 30 to 35 minutes; top with cheese during the last few minutes. Cut into squares; serve with salsa and sour cream. Makes 9 servings.

Chili Cornbread Casserole

Carolyn Deckard
Bedford, IN

My mother-in-law give me this recipe years ago, when I married my husband. It was one of his favorite dishes of hers.

8-oz. pkg. corn muffin mix
1 lb. ground beef, browned
    and drained
15-1/2 oz. can chili beans

1-3/4 oz. pkg. chili seasoning
    mix
1/2 onion, chopped
8-oz. can tomato sauce

Prepare corn muffin mix according to package instructions; set aside. In a greased 13"x9" baking pan, layer beef, chili beans, chili mix, onion and tomato sauce. Pour cornbread batter over top. Bake at 350 degrees for 30 to 35 minutes, until cornbread is done. Cut into squares to serve. Makes 6 to 8 servings.

A generous square of red-checkered
homespun makes a cozy liner for
a basket of hot rolls.

Noni's Marinara Sauce

Toni Leathers
Claremont, CA

This was the first pasta sauce my Noni taught me how to make when I was a little girl. To this day, every time I make it, which is often, the smell infuses our home, bringing back heartwarming memories of my Noni and how much I miss her. I hope you enjoy this as much as my family does!

1/4 c. olive oil
1-1/2 c. onions, finely diced
5 cloves garlic, minced
2 t. salt
1 t. pepper
1 T. dried basil

2 t. dried oregano
1/8 t. red pepper flakes
2 26-oz. containers tomato
   sauce
6-oz. tube tomato paste

In a stockpot, combine olive oil, onions, garlic, salt and pepper. Sauté over medium heat for about 10 minutes, until onions are translucent. Add basil, oregano and red pepper flakes; sauté another 5 minutes. Add tomato sauce and tomato paste; stir well. Reduce heat to low. Simmer for one to 1-1/2 hours, stirring occasionally, until flavors are well blended. Makes 10 servings.

Pasta made perfect! Bring a large pot with water to a rolling boil. Add a tablespoon of salt, if desired. Stir in pasta; return to a rolling boil. Boil, uncovered, for the time recommended on package. There's no need to add oil...frequent stirring will keep pasta from sticking together.

Mama's Baked Mostaccioli

Mia Rossi
Charlotte, NC

My grandmother made this cheesy, delicious casserole whenever we came to visit. She served it with hot garlic bread and a tomato salad fresh-picked from her garden. For dessert, we knew there would be spumoni ice cream. Such good memories!

16-oz. pkg. mostaccioli pasta, uncooked
1 lb. mild or hot Italian ground pork sausage
1 c. onion, diced
4 cloves garlic, minced

25-1/2 oz. jar pasta sauce
8-oz. pkg. shredded mozzarella cheese, divided
1/2 c. shredded Parmesan cheese, divided

Cook pasta according to package directions; drain and return to pan. Meanwhile, in a large skillet over medium heat, brown sausage with onion. Add garlic; cook for one more minute, scraping up any browned bits in the bottom of pan. Add sausage mixture and pasta sauce to cooked pasta in pan; stir well. In a greased 13"x9" baking pan, layer half of pasta mixture, half of mozzarella cheese and half of Parmesan cheese. Repeat layering, ending with cheeses. Bake, uncovered, at 350 degrees for 15 to 20 minutes, until bubbly and cheeses are melted. Let stand for 10 minutes before serving. Makes 8 servings.

A fresh salad is right at home alongside cheesy baked pasta casseroles. Toss together mixed greens, chopped tomatoes and thinly sliced red onion in a salad bowl. Whisk together 1/4 cup each of balsamic vinegar and olive oil, then drizzle over salad...so zesty!

Mom Eva's Pork Chop Casserole

Karen Richardson
Jarrettsville, MD

My mother-in-law came up with this recipe and it became a family favorite. It was on the table for dinner the night we found out we were expecting our first grandchild. If you want plenty of cabbage to go around, you can add more, as it tends to cook down. I also tend to add more garlic powder than it calls for...suit your own taste!

6 bone-in pork chops
6 to 8 c. cabbage, shredded
1 onion, thinly sliced
1/3 c. brown sugar, packed
1/4 c. cider vinegar

2 T. mustard
1/2 t. celery powder
1/2 t. garlic powder
1/2 t. chili powder

Arrange pork chops in a greased 13"x9" baking pan; cover with aluminum foil. Bake at 475 degrees for 30 minutes; remove pork chops to a plate. Spread cabbage in the bottom of pan; arrange chops over cabbage. Top chops with onion slices. In a bowl, stir together remaining ingredients; spread over pork chops and cabbage. Cover with aluminum foil. Bake at 375 degrees for 1-1/2 hours. Makes 6 servings.

A tasty apple coleslaw goes well with pork. Simply toss together a large bag of coleslaw mix, a chopped Granny Smith apple and 1/2 to one cup of mayonnaise.

Aunt Kate's Stuffed Peppers

Ann Farris
Biscoe, AR

My Aunt Kate has been gone over 20 years, but when I make any of her handed-down recipes, it's like she is in the kitchen with me. She never measured any of her creations, but I think I've finally nailed this recipe. This is so easy, but makes a beautiful plated supper.

6 green peppers, tops cut off
   and reserved
2 to 3 t. oil
1 lb. cooked ham, finely diced

1 onion, finely diced
1 c. cooked rice
1 t. pepper
1 c. shredded Cheddar cheese

Place pepper shells upside-down on paper towels to drain. Dice reserved pepper tops, measuring out 1/2 cup. In a skillet over medium heat, combine oil, diced peppers, ham, onion and cooked rice. Cook until vegetables are tender. Season with pepper. Spoon mixture into peppers; place peppers in a lightly greased 13"x9" glass baking pan. Pour 1/4-inch water into pan. Bake, uncovered, at 325 degrees for about 30 minutes. During the last 5 minutes, top with cheese. Return to oven and bake until cheese is melted. Makes 6 servings.

Encourage children to take a no-thank-you helping,
or just one bite, of foods they think they don't like...
they may be pleasantly surprised!

Grandma's Best COMFORT FOODS

Skillet Beef & Rice

Georgia Muth
Penn Valley, CA

*This festive skillet recipe was given to me by a dear neighbor over
40 years ago. I serve it with a tossed green salad and warm tortillas.
For an extra kick, add a little hot sauce or salsa.*

1 T. oil
1 lb. ground beef
3 T. onion, diced
1/2 c. green pepper, diced
3 T. celery, diced
1-1/3 c. instant rice, uncooked
2 8-oz. cans tomato sauce

1 c. hot water
1 cube beef bouillon
1 t. soy sauce
1 t. sugar
1 c. shredded Cheddar cheese
Garnish: snipped fresh parsley

Heat oil in a skillet over medium heat; brown beef with onion, green
pepper and celery. Stir in uncooked rice, tomato sauce, hot water,
bouillon cube, soy sauce and sugar. Cover and simmer for 8 to
10 minutes, until rice is tender. Serve hot, topped with shredded
cheese and parsley. Makes 4 to 6 servings.

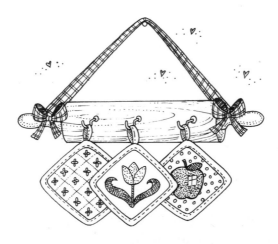

Make a handy potholder rack from a vintage wooden rolling pin.
Place a row of cup hooks along one side and add a strip
of homespun tied to each end for hanging. So simple!

COMFORT FOOD
Dinner Classics

Gram's Cheeseburger Casserole
Anne Ptacnik
Yuma, CO

*When I was in high school, we had an open campus for lunchtime.
Since I was a country kid, I was blessed to be able to often eat lunch
with my grandparents, who lived in my hometown. Sometimes,
Grandma would have this quick stovetop meal ready for me. It's way
better than a boxed burger dinner, and I usually have all the
ingredients on hand. Make it a complete meal with warm rolls and
a tossed salad.*

1 lb. ground beef
1/2 c. onion, diced
1-1/2 c. water
1/2 c. catsup
2 T. mustard

1/2 t. salt
1/4 t. pepper
1-1/2 c. instant rice, uncooked
1 c. shredded Cheddar cheese

Brown beef and onion in a large skillet over medium heat; drain. Stir in
water, catsup, mustard, salt and pepper. Bring to a boil; stir in uncooked
rice. Cover and remove from heat. Let stand for 5 minutes. Fluff with a
fork; sprinkle with cheese. Cover and let stand until cheese melts.
Makes 4 to 6 servings.

A Lazy Susan is so handy for keeping canned soups, vegetables and
other pantry staples at your fingertips. Just give it a quick spin
to bring the item you need to the front of the cupboard.

Missouri Skillet Luau

Carolyn Deckard
Bedford, IN

My family always asks for this recipe to be fixed for special family gatherings. It is something everyone likes, which doesn't happen often!

1 lb. ground beef
1 egg, beaten
1/4 c. dry bread crumbs
1/4 t. ground ginger
1/2 t. salt
1/4 c. all-purpose flour
1 T. oil
20-oz. can pineapple chunks,
    drained and juice reserved

1/4 c. vinegar
3 T. brown sugar, packed
1 T. soy sauce
3/4 t. cornstarch
2 green peppers, cut into strips
hot buttered noodles

In a large bowl, mix beef with egg, bread crumbs and seasonings. Mix well and form into 16 meatballs; roll in flour. Brown in oil in a large skillet over medium heat. Remove meatballs to a plate, reserving drippings in skillet. Add enough water to reserved pineapple juice to make one cup; stir into drippings in skillet. In a cup, mix vinegar, brown sugar, soy sauce and cornstarch; add to mixture in skillet. Cook, stirring constantly, until sauce is thickened and clear. Return meatballs to skillet; add pineapple chunks and green pepper strips in sauce. Cover and simmer over low heat for 10 minutes. Serve meatballs and sauce over hot buttered noodles. Serves 6 to 8.

A refreshing beverage for a spicy supper! Combine equal amounts of ginger ale and pineapple juice and pour into ice-filled tumblers. Garnish with fresh fruit slices stacked up on drinking straws.

COMFORT FOOD
Dinner Classics

Chicken & Peaches

Theresa Long
Arnoldsville, GA

My mom used to make this delicious dish. People were never sure about the combination until they tried it, and then they always loved it, especially the warm biscuits on the top.

1/4 c. oil
1 t. butter, melted
1 c. all-purpose flour
1/2 c. milk
2 eggs, beaten
8 bone-in chicken thighs or
   6 chicken breasts

garlic salt, salt and pepper
   to taste
15-1/4 oz. can sliced peaches
   in heavy syrup
16.3-oz. tube refrigerated flaky
   biscuits

Spread oil and melted butter in the bottom of a 3-quart casserole dish; set aside. Add flour to a shallow bowl; whisk together milk and eggs in a separate bowl. Roll chicken pieces in flour, then in egg mixture, then in flour again. Arrange chicken in casserole dish; sprinkle with seasonings. Bake, uncovered, at 400 degrees for 30 minutes, or until chicken is turning golden. Spoon peaches and syrup over chicken. Arrange biscuits in dish, pushing them down into drippings. Bake for another 12 to 15 minutes, until biscuits are golden and chicken juices run clear. Makes 4 to 6 servings.

Shopping for canned peaches to use in a recipe? Look for old-fashioned canned freestone peaches...they're closest to home-canned.

Grandma's Best
COMFORT FOODS

Presto Chicken Pesto

Amy Thomason Hunt
Traphill, NC

This dish tastes like you cooked with your grandma all day!

16-oz. pkg. favorite pasta,
  uncooked
4 boneless, skinless chicken
  breasts
1-1/2 T. olive oil
12-oz. jar chicken gravy

1/4 c. water
2 T. jarred pesto sauce
2 t. lemon juice
Garnish: shredded Parmesan
  cheese

Cook pasta according to package directions; drain. Meanwhile, in a large skillet over medium heat, brown chicken in olive oil. Cover and cook for 8 minutes, or until cooked through. Remove chicken to a plate; cover to keep warm. To drippings in skillet, add gravy, water, pesto and lemon juice. Heat through, stirring often. Serve chicken over cooked pasta. Cover with sauce from skillet; sprinkle with cheese. Makes 4 servings.

Instant Pierogie Casserole

Shannon Reents
Poland, OH

This an easy dish my mom used to make when I was a little girl.

6 to 8 lasagna noodles, uncooked
8-oz. pkg. instant mashed potato
  flakes, uncooked
3 onions, chopped

1/2 c. butter
1-1/2 to 2 c. pasteurized process
  cheese, cubed

Cook noodles according to package directions; drain. Prepare instant potatoes according to package directions; set aside. In a skillet over medium heat, sauté onions in butter until translucent. In a greased 13"x9" baking pan, layer half each of noodles, potatoes and cheese. Repeat layering, ending with cheese. Top with onion mixture. Bake, uncovered, at 350 degrees for 25 to 30 minutes, until hot and bubbly. Makes 6 to 8 servings.

For a crispy, golden topping, leave the casserole dish uncovered while it's baking.

COMFORT FOOD
Dinner Classics

Chicken Surprise

Anita Polizzi
Bakersville, NC

My mother-in-law made this recipe to feed lots of family members. The kids loved it. It was always a surprise to see what piece of chicken you got as you unwrapped the foil.

3/4 c. butter, melted, or more
   as needed
2 to 3 c. Italian-seasoned
   dry bread crumbs or
   panko crumbs

4 chicken breasts, thighs
   or drumsticks

Tear 4 long sheets of aluminum foil; set aside. Add melted butter to a shallow bowl; add bread crumbs to a separate bowl. Dip chicken pieces into melted butter; dredge in bread crumbs. Place each piece of chicken on a piece of foil; drizzle with at least one tablespoon butter. Wrap and seal foil well; place packets on a baking sheet. Bake at 350 degrees, about 40 to 45 minutes for chicken breasts, less time for thighs and drumsticks. At serving time, let each person choose their surprise piece. Makes 4 servings.

Keep a picnic basket packed with a blanket, tableware and other picnic supplies. You'll be ready to pack up an easy-to-tote casserole dinner, load everyone into the car and take off for a picnic at a moment's notice!

Grandma's Best
COMFORT FOODS

Cheesy Mini Meatloaves

Debra Arch
Kewanee, IL

My children would always brag about these cheesy individual meatloaves whenever Grandma made them during sleep-over visits to her house. I don't know where she first got this recipe, but it is very tasty and can be made with ingredients that most people already have on hand in the kitchen. These yummy meatloaves taste even better the next day...if you have any left over!

1-1/2 lbs. ground beef
1 onion, chopped
2 eggs, beaten
1 c. long-cooking oats, uncooked
1 c. milk

1 c. shredded Cheddar cheese
1 c. catsup
1/3 c. brown sugar, packed
1 T. mustard

In a large bowl, mix together beef, onion, eggs, oats, milk and cheese; form into 12 balls. Arrange meatballs in a greased 13"x9" baking pan. In a small bowl, stir together remaining ingredients; spread 2/3 of mixture over meatballs. Cover with aluminum foil. Bake at 350 degrees for one hour. Remove from oven; uncover and spoon remaining sauce over meatballs. Bake, uncovered, for 15 to 20 minutes more. Makes 6 servings, 2 meatballs each.

First aid for a casserole dish with baked-on food spatters!
Mix equal amounts of cream of tartar and white vinegar into
a paste. Spread onto the dish and let stand for 30 minutes
to an hour. Spatters will wash off easily.

COMFORT FOOD
Dinner Classics

Cheesy Rice & Beans

Leslie Harvie
Simpsonville, SC

My mom made this quite often when I was young, and it was always one of my favorite meals. Recently, I was thrilled to find it written in the back of one of her cookbooks. The ingredients are simple, but it is so delicious!

3 c. cooked brown rice
15-1/2 oz. can kidney beans,
   drained
1 c. yellow onion, chopped

3 cloves garlic, minced
1 t. salt
1 c. ricotta cheese
3 c. shredded Cheddar cheese

In a large bowl, combine cooked rice, beans, onion, garlic and salt. In a lightly greased 13"x9" baking pan, layer half of rice mixture, half of ricotta cheese and half of Cheddar cheese. Repeat layering. Bake, uncovered, at 350 degrees for 30 minutes, or until bubbly and golden. Makes 8 servings.

Simple Salsa Chicken

Sara Stoker
North Logan, UT

This slow-cooker recipe reminds me of my grandma's house. Always good-smelling and delicious...a family favorite! It is so easy, you will love it too.

2 to 4 boneless, skinless
   chicken breasts
16-oz. jar favorite salsa
15-1/2 oz. can Great Northern
   beans, drained

15-1/2 oz. can black beans,
   drained
Garnish: favorite shredded
   cheese
Optional: tortilla chips

Spray a 5-quart slow cooker with non-stick vegetable spray; add chicken. Top with salsa and beans. Cover and cook on low setting for 6 to 8 hours, until chicken is very tender. Shred chicken and stir into mixture in slow cooker. Serve topped with shredded cheese, spooned over tortilla chips if desired. Makes 2 to 4 servings.

Grandma's Best
COMFORT FOODS

Mom's World's Best Tacos

 Jennifer Blay
Puyallup, WA

I hope you enjoy this awesome taco recipe with your loved ones...they are the best tacos I've ever had! The smell of them simmering away on the stove brings back such good memories of Mom making them for me. My good friend Brandi hated tacos, but she tried these, and now these are the only tacos she will eat. Try using ground chicken or turkey breast instead of beef too.

1 lb. ground beef
16-oz. jar hot, medium,
   or mild salsa
4-oz. can diced green chiles
16-oz. can refried beans

corn taco shells or tortillas
Garnish: shredded lettuce, diced
   tomatoes, shredded Cheddar
   cheese, taco sauce, sour
   cream, guacamole

Brown beef in a large skillet over medium heat; drain. Stir in salsa and chiles; bring to a boil. Reduce heat to medium-low; cover and simmer for 20 to 25 minutes. Stir in refried beans. Continue cooking, uncovered, over medium-low heat for 10 to 15 more minutes. To serve, spoon a generous amount of beef mixture into each taco shell or tortilla; add desired toppings. Serves 4 to 6.

Salsa in a jiffy! Pour a can of stewed tomatoes, several slices of canned jalapeño pepper and a teaspoon or two of the jalapeño juice into a blender. Add a little chopped onion, if you like. Cover and process to the desired consistency.

COMFORT FOOD
Dinner Classics

Granny Doris's Chile Rellenos Casserole

Tammy Navarro
Littleton, CO

My late mother-in-law, whom I loved with all my heart, gave me this recipe. It was her favorite. Serve with Spanish rice and refried beans on the side.

27-oz. can whole Hatch green
    chiles, drained
3/4 lb. ground beef chuck
1/4 c. onion, chopped
4 eggs
1 c. whole milk

1/4 c. all-purpose flour
1/4 t. salt
1/8 t. pepper
1-1/2 c. shredded Colby
    Jack cheese

Split chiles and remove seeds; dry chiles on paper towels. Brown beef with onion in a skillet over medium heat; drain. Beat eggs in a bowl; whisk in milk, flour, salt and pepper. Arrange peppers in a sprayed 13"x9" baking pan; sprinkle with cheese. Spoon beef mixture over cheese and peppers; pour batter over beef. Bake, uncovered, at 350 degrees for 45 to 50 minutes, until heated through and a knife tip inserted in the center comes out clean. Serves 8.

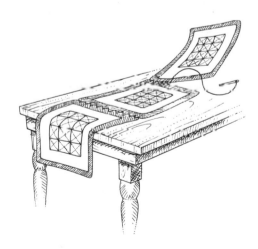

Whip up a country-style table runner in a jiffy! Just stitch several quilted placemats end-to-end.

Grandma's Best
COMFORT FOODS

Chicken Paprikash

Patricia Owens
Vermilion, OH

This recipe is from my maternal grandmother, who emigrated from Hungary in 1906. I've been making it since I was a teenager. Whenever I make it I think about her. It's my favorite comfort food.

2 T. shortening
1 c. onion, sliced
2 T. Hungarian paprika
1 t. salt
3 lbs. bone-in chicken pieces

1 to 2 14-1/2 oz. cans chicken
   broth
1 c. sour cream
1/4 c. cornstarch

Melt shortening in a large skillet over medium heat. Add onion and sauté until tender. Add seasonings; mix well. Add chicken to skillet; cook until lightly golden on both sides. Add enough chicken broth to skillet to nearly cover chicken. Cover and simmer over medium-low heat for about 45 minutes, until chicken is tender. Remove chicken to a plate, reserving broth in skillet; set aside. Meanwhile, make and cook Dumplings; set aside. In a small bowl, combine sour cream, cornstarch and a little of the cooking juices from skillet. Mix until smooth; add to broth in skillet. Cook and stir over high heat for a few minutes, until smooth and thickened. Return chicken pieces to sauce in skillet, discarding bones and skin if desired. Serve chicken and sauce over dumplings. Makes 4 to 5 servings.

Dumplings:

6 eggs
1 c. water

1 t. salt
5-1/2 to 6 c. all-purpose flour

Beat eggs in a large bowl. Add water and salt; mix well. Gradually add flour, mixing well until a stiff dough forms. Drop dough by teaspoonfuls into a saucepan of boiling water; cook for about 10 minutes. Drain; rinse with cold water.

Grandma Boca's Rice

Phyllis Mayle
Hubbard, OH

When I was a child, my grandmother would make this dish
whenever she had some leftover spaghetti sauce. I loved it
as a child and still do. Now I make it for my own family.

2 lbs. ground beef
4-oz. can sliced mushrooms,
   drained
1/4 c. onion, diced

2 32-oz. jars spaghetti sauce
3 c. cooked instant rice
1 t. salt
pepper to taste

In a large, deep skillet over medium heat, lightly brown beef with
mushrooms and onion; drain. Spoon spaghetti sauce over beef mixture;
add enough water to cover beef. Simmer over medium-low heat for
30 minutes, stirring occasionally. Stir in cooked rice, salt and pepper;
mixture should be more soupy than thick. Heat through over low
heat; if sauce thickens, add a little more water. Freezes well. Makes
6 servings.

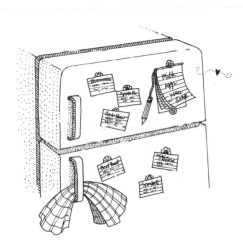

Create mini recipe cards listing the ingredients of favorite
one-dish dinners. Glue a button magnet on the back and
place on the fridge...so handy whenever it's time to make
out a shopping list!

Potato Puff Casserole

Sandie Bins
Vancouver, WA

*This recipe has been handed down from my great-grandma. My
mother taught me how to make it when I was just ten years old!
We have a very big family and it always fills everyone up.*

1 lb. ground beef
2 10-3/4 oz. cans cream of
   mushroom soup
1-1/4 c. milk

14-1/2 oz. can corn, drained
28-oz. pkg. frozen potato puffs,
   divided
salt and pepper to taste

Cook beef in a large skillet over medium heat until no longer pink;
drain. Add soup and milk; mix well. Cook over medium heat until
slightly thickened, stirring occasionally. Add corn and stir well. Arrange
half of potato puffs in a greased 13"x9" baking pan to cover bottom of
pan. Spoon beef mixture over potato puffs, spreading to cover very well;
season with salt and pepper. Cover with remaining potato puffs. Cover
tightly with aluminum foil. Bake on center oven rack at 350 degrees
for one hour. Remove foil; increase oven to 400 degrees. Bake another
15 to 20 minutes, until puffs are lightly golden. Let stand 5 minutes at
room temperature before serving. Serves 4 to 6.

Ingredient swaps are easy with most casserole recipes. If there's
no cream of mushroom soup in the pantry, cream of chicken
or celery is sure to be tasty too.

COMFORT FOOD
Dinner Classics

Weiner Goulash

Terri Lotz-Ganley
South Euclid, OH

My son and I love, love, love hot dogs! This recipe was one of my grandmother's that she came up with during the Depression. It was one of my favorites when I was little and is still a favorite today. When my son was little, he loved it too...he called it hot dog soup! Serve with a crisp tossed salad.

3/4 c. butter, sliced
3/4 c. onion, chopped
3 15-oz. pkgs. bun-size hot
    dogs, cut into one-inch pieces

paprika to taste
4 to 5 redskin potatoes, cut into
    one to 2-inch cubes
salt and pepper to taste

Melt butter in a large, deep saucepan over medium heat. Add onion and sauté until translucent. Add hot dogs; sprinkle generously with enough paprika to cover them. Mix well. Cook, stirring often, until hot dogs are lightly browned and ends puff out slightly. Add potatoes; season with salt and pepper. Add enough water to cover potatoes by about 1/2 inch; mix well. Cover and bring to a boil. Reduce heat to medium-low and simmer for 30 minutes, stirring occasionally Makes 6 to 8 servings.

Gramma's Casserole

Suellen Anderson
Rockford, IL

My folks raised seven kids, so Mom had to be creative with ground beef. This is always the dish all 22 grandkids love the most!

2 to 3 baking potatoes, peeled
    and sliced
1 to 2 T. water
1 lb. ground beef, browned
    and drained

2 10-3/4 oz. cans vegetable
    beef soup

Layer potatoes in a greased 3-quart casserole dish; sprinkle with water. Spread browned beef over potatoes; spoon soup over beef. Cover and bake at 350 degrees for 40 to 60 minutes, until heated through and potatoes are fork-tender. Makes 8 servings.

Grandma's Best
COMFORT FOODS

Oven "Fried" Chicken

Sandra Mirando
Depew, NY

This is such an easy and delicious recipe...and a great use for buttermilk.

10 boneless chicken thighs
2 c. buttermilk
1/4 c. lemon juice
4 t. Worcestershire sauce
4 t. celery seed
2 t. paprika
4 t. salt

1/2 t. pepper
1 clove garlic, minced,
   or 1/8 t. garlic powder
2 to 3 c. Italian-seasoned dry
   bread crumbs
1/2 c. butter, melted

Place chicken in a one-gallon plastic zipping bag; set aside. In a bowl, combine remaining ingredients except bread crumbs and butter; mix well and add to bag with chicken. Seal bag; turn to coat well. Refrigerate overnight, turning bag occasionally. Drain, discarding marinade. Coat chicken in bread crumbs; place in a greased 13"x9" baking pan. Drizzle melted butter over chicken. Bake, uncovered, at 350 degrees for one hour, or until bubbly and chicken juices run clear when pierced. Serves 6 to 8.

The aroma of dinner baking in the oven is so cozy and inviting on a chilly day...why not make it a whole oven meal? Roasted vegetables and homemade rolls can easily bake alongside your main dish. Yum!

Chicken & Wild Rice

Janice Curtis
Yucaipa, CA

This is a great dish, good for having company over or for taking to potluck dinners. It's easy to put together...I make it even easier by using rotisserie chicken.

6-oz. pkg. long-grain and wild rice, uncooked
3 c. cooked chicken, cubed
14-1/2 oz. can cut green beans, drained
8-oz. can water chestnuts, drained and minced
3/4 c. onion, minced
10-3/4 oz. can cream of celery soup
1/2 c. mayonnaise
1/2 c. sour cream
1/2 c. grated Parmesan cheese or shredded Cheddar cheese

Prepare rice according to package directions; set aside to cool. In a large bowl, combine remaining ingredients except cheese; add cooked rice and mix well. Transfer to a greased 2-quart casserole dish; top with cheese. Bake, uncovered, at 350 degrees for 35 to 40 minutes, until hot and bubbly. Makes 6 to 8 servings.

Serve some savory garlic twists with dinner. Separate refrigerated bread stick dough and lay flat on an ungreased baking sheet. Brush with olive oil; sprinkle with garlic salt and dried parsley. Give each bread stick a twist or two and bake as directed on the package.

Grandma's Best
COMFORT FOODS

Slow-Cooker Brisket

Angie Miller
Wichita Falls, TX

This was my great-grandmother's recipe. Over the years, I've played with it and adjusted some different things in it. It's really delicious, with very little effort. Serve with your favorite potatoes.

3 t. garlic powder, divided
2 t. chili powder
1/2 t. paprika
2 t. salt
1/2 t. pepper
4 to 5-lb. beef brisket

1/2 c. catsup
1/3 c. cider vinegar
1/4 c. brown sugar, packed
2 T. Worcestershire sauce
2 t. Dijon mustard

In a cup, combine 2 teaspoons garlic powder and remaining seasonings; mix well and rub over brisket. Place brisket in a 6-quart slow cooker sprayed with non-stick vegetable spray; set aside. In a small bowl, whisk together remaining garlic powder and other ingredients; spoon over brisket. Cover and cook on low setting for 7 to 8 hours, until tender. Serves 4 to 6.

Mashed potatoes are the perfect side dish for pot roast
and gravy. Try a delicious secret the next time you fix the
potatoes...substitute equal parts chicken broth and
cream for the milk in any favorite recipe.

COMFORT FOOD
Dinner Classics

Mom's Liver & Onions

Denise Herr
West Jefferson, OH

You may convert some non-liver eaters with this recipe! Soaking the liver in milk helps reduce the strong liver taste. The biscuit mix is slightly sweet and makes this just delicious.

1-1/2 lb. container chicken livers
    or calves' liver, sliced
1 c. milk
2 T. butter, divided
2 T. oil, divided

1 onion, thinly sliced
1 c. biscuit baking mix
10-1/2 oz. can French onion
    soup
salt and pepper to taste

In a bowl, cover liver with milk; let stand for 10 minutes. Meanwhile, in a skillet over medium heat, melt one tablespoon butter with one tablespoon oil. Add onion and cook until golden; transfer to a greased 2-quart casserole dish. Add remaining butter and oil to same skillet. Remove liver from milk; dredge in biscuit mix and add to skillet. Sauté liver until golden, turning several times. Transfer liver to casserole dish, placing over onion; pour onion soup over all. Season with salt and pepper. Cover and bake at 350 degrees for 25 minutes, or until liver is tender and no longer pink in the center. Serves 6.

Stir seasoned salt and coarse pepper into some flour, and fill a big shaker to keep by the side of the stove. So handy to sprinkle on meat for pan-frying!

Stovetop Scalloped Potatoes & Ham

Karen Antonides
Gahanna, OH

I have been using this recipe for years. Cooked potatoes, mixed with ham and topped with a creamy sauce, equal the ideal comfort food on a cold winter day. Delicious and comforting...the leftovers are wonderful too, if you have any!

8 to 10 potatoes, peeled
    and cubed
1 T. butter, melted
2 T. all-purpose flour
1 c. milk
1-1/8 t. dry mustard

1 t. onion powder
1/2 t. garlic powder
1/2 t. salt
1/2 t. pepper
2 c. cooked ham, cubed

In a saucepan, cover potatoes with water. Bring to a boil over high heat; boil until tender. Drain, reserving one cup of cooking water. Transfer potatoes to a 3-quart casserole dish; set aside. Melt butter in another saucepan over medium heat. Sprinkle with flour; cook and stir until blended. Add reserved potato water; bring to a gentle boil while stirring constantly. Add milk and seasonings; continue cooking at a gentle boil, stirring constantly, until thickened. Add ham and sauce to potatoes; mix well and serve. Makes 6 to 8 servings.

Keep a shaker canister of quick-mixing flour on hand for dusting pork chops, cubes of stew beef or other meat before browning. It blends well with flour in sauces too.

COMFORT FOOD
Dinner Classics

Hot Chicken Salad

JoAlice Patterson-Welton
Lawrenceville, GA

This has been a favorite family hand-me-down recipe for many years.
I got it from my late mom, who was a fabulous Southern cook. I never
met a dish of Mom's that I didn't like!

5 boneless, skinless chicken
    breasts, cooked and diced
2 10-3/4 oz. cans cream of
    chicken soup
10-3/4 oz. can cream of
    celery soup
1-1/2 c. mayonnaise

1-1/2 c. celery, chopped
1-1/2 c. onion, chopped
2-1/4 oz. pkg. slivered almonds
5 T. lemon juice
1-1/2 c. sharp Cheddar cheese
salt and pepper to taste
3 c. potato chips, crushed

In a bowl, mix together all ingredients except potato chips, adding salt
and pepper to taste. Spread in a greased 13"x9" baking pan; top with
crushed chips. Bake, uncovered, at 375 degrees for 15 to 20 minutes.
until hot and bubbly. Serves 6 to 8.

Creamy Chicken Breasts

Judy Henfey
Cibolo, TX

An easy dinner for the holiday season, or anytime!
Serve over cooked rice...scrumptious.

6 to 8 boneless, skinless chicken
    breasts
1/2 c. margarine
2/3 c. onion, chopped

1 clove garlic, minced
1-1/2 c. half-and-half
4 t. Worcestershire sauce
1/2 t. pepper

In a skillet over medium heat, cook chicken in margarine until golden on
both sides. Arrange chicken in a single layer in a greased 13"x9" baking
pan; set aside. Add onion and garlic to drippings in skillet; sauté until
tender. Add half-and-half, Worcestershire sauce and pepper, stirring to
scrape up the brown bits in skillet. Spoon sauce over chicken. Cover
tightly; bake at 325 degrees for 2 hours, or until chicken is very tender.
Makes 6 to 8 servings.

Mom's Spaghetti

Robin Younkin
Monterey, CA

I grew up enjoying this spaghetti with its secret ingredient...instant coffee. My husband is half-Italian and this is the only spaghetti recipe we make. It's addictive! My friends would be skeptical at first, but a few days later would ask for the recipe so that they could make it at home. Be sure to bake up some garlic bread on the side, as the sauce is especially delicious with it.

1 T. olive oil or butter	1/2 t. salt
6 cloves garlic, minced	1/4 t. pepper
1 red onion, chopped	2 T. instant coffee granules
1 lb. ground beef	1/2 c. warm water
10-3/4 oz. can tomato soup	16-oz. pkg spaghetti, cooked
6-oz. can tomato paste	Garnish: grated Parmesan cheese

In a large pot, heat oil or butter over medium heat. Add garlic and onion; cook until fragrant. Add beef; cook and stir just until no pink remains. Drain; stir in tomato soup, tomato paste, salt and pepper. In a cup, dissolve instant coffee in warm water; add to beef mixture. Cook over medium heat for 30 minutes, stirring occasionally. For richer flavor, allow the sauce to simmer longer. Serve cooked spaghetti topped with a generous ladle of sauce and some Parmesan cheese. Serves 8.

Make some warm Parmesan bread for supper. Blend 1/4 cup butter with 2 tablespoons grated Parmesan cheese, 2 teaspoons minced garlic and 1/4 teaspoon Italian seasoning. Spread it over the cut sides of a French bread and broil until golden. Yum!

Taco Spaghetti

Sandra Turner
Fayetteville, NC

This recipe has been enjoyed by four generations of our family, ages 2-1/2 to 86. I love that it is made all in one pot, so clean-up is super easy. I like to measure all the seasonings together in a bowl before starting, so that I can add them all at once after the beef is cooked.

1 lb. ground beef
3 T. tomato paste
1-oz. pkg. taco seasoning mix
1 T. dried, minced onions
1 t. chili powder
1/2 t. garlic salt
28-oz. can crushed tomatoes

10-oz. can diced tomatoes with green chiles
16-oz. pkg. thin spaghetti, uncooked and broken in half
4 c. beef broth
1/2 c. whipping cream

In a Dutch oven over medium heat, cook beef until no longer pink. Drain; stir in tomato paste, taco seasoning, onions and seasonings. Cook for one or 2 minutes to blend flavors. Add tomatoes with juice, uncooked spaghetti, beef broth and cream; stir well. Bring to a boil; reduce heat to medium-low. Simmer for 15 to 20 minutes, stirring occasionally. Makes 6 servings.

Put those handed-down cut-glass coasters to new use as holders for fat pillar candles. Group several together for a glowing centerpiece in an instant.

Grandma's Best
COMFORT FOODS

Kielbasa & Potatoes

Doreen Knapp
Stanfordville, NY

When I was growing up, my mom used to make this for us as a quick weeknight meal. Now I make this for my family too. I still love it and now my older son loves it also. Serve with buttered bread and a crisp side salad.

7 russet potatoes, peeled
   and cubed
2 14-oz. pkgs. Kielbasa or
   beef smoked sausage, cubed
1/4 c. oil
2 green peppers, chopped

1 c. onion, diced
1/4 t. garlic powder
1/4 t. onion powder
salt and pepper to taste
9-oz. pkg. frozen peas

Add potatoes to a large microwave-safe bowl. Cover with plastic wrap and microwave on high for 8 minutes. Stir; microwave for another 8 to 12 minutes, until knife-tender. Meanwhile, add Kielbasa and oil to a large skillet over medium heat; sauté until browned. Remove Kielbasa to a large bowl, reserving drippings in pan. Add potatoes, peppers and onion to skillet and sauté until golden; drain. Return Kielbasa to skillet; add seasonings and stir well. Add peas; cook until peas are soft and warmed through. Serves 4 to 6.

Thank God for dirty dishes,
They have a tale to tell.
While others may go hungry,
We're eating very well.
–Author Unknown

COMFORT FOOD
Dinner Classics

Hot Dog Hash

Dina Willard
Abingdon, MD

This is one of those delicious recipes that happens when you need to clean out your pantry! Very easy and my family loves it.

1 to 2 T. oil
16-oz. pkg. hot dogs,
    cut into thirds
1 c. frozen peppers and onions
2 bags boil-in-bag rice, uncooked
28-oz. can whole tomatoes

1/2 c. molasses
1/2 c. brown sugar, packed
1 T. mustard
15-1/2 oz. can red beans,
    drained
15-1/2 oz. white beans, drained

Heat oil in a large stockpot over medium heat. Cook hot dogs with frozen vegetables for 3 to 4 minutes, just until browned. Meanwhile, cook rice according to package directions; drain. In a bowl, combine tomatoes with juice, molasses, brown sugar and mustard. Stir until blended; pour over hot dog mixture. Add cooked rice and remaining ingredients; bring to a boil. Reduce heat to medium-low. Simmer for 20 to 25 minutes, until bubbly and sauce is heated through. Makes 4 to 6 servings.

Grandma's Meat Pie

Donna Moore
East Bernard, TX

My grandmother would make this when she knew we were coming. Sometimes, as a little girl, I got to help her chop the vegetables!

2 9-inch pie crusts, unbaked
1 lb. ground beef
3 potatoes, peeled and finely
    chopped

2 carrots, peeled and finely
    chopped
1/2 c. onion, finely chopped
salt and pepper to taste

Place one pie crust in a 9" pie plate; set aside. In a large bowl, mix uncooked beef and vegetables well; season with salt and pepper. Press mixture into crust in pan; cover with remaining pie crust. Press to seal edges; cut several slits with a knife tip. Bake at 350 degrees for one hour, or until golden. Cut into wedges. Serves 8.

Runzas

Christine Gordon
Derby, KS

This is a dish that I grew up eating in Nebraska as a kid. The recipe was passed down to my mom. She received it from my grandmother, who learned it from a friend who was Slavic. The recipe calls for frozen bread dough, but feel free to use your own homemade bread dough, if you prefer.

2-loaf pkg. frozen white or
   wheat bread dough
1 lb. ground beef
1/2 onion, chopped

1 head cabbage, shredded, or
   16-oz. pkg. shredded
   coleslaw mix
salt and pepper to taste

Thaw bread dough according to package instructions. Meanwhile, in a skillet over medium heat, brown beef with onion. Drain; add cabbage, salt and pepper. Cook and stir over medium heat for 5 to 8 minutes, until cabbage is slightly wilted and cooked down. Set aside to cool slightly. On a floured surface, roll out dough into a rectangle, about 1/3 to 1/4 inch thick. With a pizza cutter or knife, cut dough into hand-sized squares. Spoon 3 to 4 tablespoons of beef mixture into the center of each square. Bring the 4 corners together; pinch completely closed. Place stuffed rolls seam-side down on a greased baking sheet. Bake at 350 degrees for about 12 to 15 minutes, until golden. Makes 1-1/2 to 2 dozen rolls; serves 6 to 8.

While the main dish bakes, turn leftover mashed potatoes into twice-baked potatoes. Stir in minced onion, crumbled bacon, sour cream and shredded cheese to taste. Pat into mini casserole dishes. Bake at 350 degrees until hot and golden...scrumptious!

COMFORT FOOD
Dinner Classics

Grandmother's American Chop Suey

*Janae Mallonee
Marlboro, MA*

My grandmother, my mother and I make this dish all the time. It's cheap, simple, and a great weeknight meal. Every time I bite into it, I am 6 years old again and everything is simple! I was watching a cooking show on TV and they were talking about this recipe...and apparently it is only a New England food? Being local, it never entered my mind that not everyone was eating this same meal!

16-oz. pkg. elbow macaroni,
   uncooked
1 lb. lean ground beef
1 onion, chopped

1 green pepper, chopped
2 10-3/4 oz. cans tomato soup
salt and pepper to taste
grated Parmesan cheese to taste

Cook macaroni according to package directions; drain and return to cooking pot. Meanwhile, in a large skillet over medium-high heat, sauté beef with onion and green pepper for 5 to 10 minutes, until beef is browned and crumbly. Drain; add tomato soup and stir well to combine. Add beef mixture to cooked macaroni in pot. Mix well and season with salt, pepper and Parmesan cheese. Serve topped with additional cheese. Makes 5 servings.

Start a kitchen journal that's part cookbook, part keepsake. Decorate a blank book, then write or paste in recipes you've tried. Add notes about everyone's favorites and who was visiting for dinner. You'll love looking back on these happy memories!

Chicken Shortcake

Cassandra Gleason
Fond du Lac, WI

This is an old recipe my mother handed down to me. It's fairly simple, very similar to chicken and milk gravy served over cornbread. Use baked or poached chicken as you like.

3 T. butter
3 T. all-purpose flour
1-1/2 c. milk
1/2 t. salt

1/4 t. pepper
3 boneless, skinless chicken
    breasts, cooked and diced

Prepare and bake Shortcake; cool. Melt butter in a large saucepan over medium heat. Stir in flour and cook for a few minutes, stirring constantly. Slowly add milk, stirring constantly. Cook and stir until thick and creamy; add salt and pepper. Stir in cooked chicken. Cook over low heat for 5 minutes, adding more milk if sauce is too thick. Serve creamed chicken over squares of shortcake. Serves 4.

Shortcake:

1/4 c. plus 1 T. shortening,
    divided
1 c. cornmeal
1 c. all-purpose flour
1 T. baking powder

1 t. sugar
1/4 t. salt
1 egg, beaten
1 c. buttermilk

Coat an 8"x8" baking pan with one tablespoon shortening; set in oven at 425 degrees to heat. In a bowl, combine cornmeal, flour, baking powder, sugar and salt; mix well. Add remaining shortening, egg and buttermilk; stir just until combined. Remove pan from oven; pour batter into pan. Bake at 425 degrees for 20 minutes; cool and cut into squares.

There is nothing wrong with the world that a sensible woman
could not settle in an afternoon.
–Jean Giraudoux

FAMILY &
FRIENDS
Get-Together

Grandma's Best
COMFORT FOODS

Parmesan Party Log

Carolyn Deckard
Bedford, IN

This tasty recipe has been in our family for years. It's something different to serve at showers and other parties. A good make-ahead!

8-oz. pkg. cream cheese,
   softened
1/2 c. grated Parmesan cheese
1/4 t. onion salt or garlic salt

2 T. green pepper, chopped
2 T. diced pimentos, drained
Garnish: chopped fresh parsley

In a bowl, combine cream cheese, Parmesan cheese and salt; mix until well blended. Add green pepper and pimentos; mix well. Cover and chill. At serving time, form into a log shape; coat with chopped parsley. May be made a few days ahead and kept refrigerated. Makes 8 servings.

Repurpose Grandma's collection of canning jars. They're perfect for serving frosty cold beverages at casual get-togethers with family & friends.

Weenies & Bacon

Patricia Nicley
Washburn, TN

When I was growing up, my mother and grandmother would make these. Wherever I have taken these, everyone loves them! My husband and sons don't like sweet pickles, so I make some without pickles for them.

1 lb. hot dogs
2 to 3 slices Cheddar cheese,
   cut into strips

Optional: 1/4 c. sweet pickles,
   diced
8 to 10 slices bacon

Split hot dogs down the center, but not all the way through. Fill each hot dog with a cheese strip and some pickles; wrap with a slice of bacon. Place in an ungreased 9"x9" glass baking pan. Bake, uncovered, at 350 degrees for 30 minutes, until cheese is melted and bacon is crisp. Makes 8 to 10 servings.

Sausage-Stuffed Mushrooms

Kimberly (Mimi) Kuhn
Lake Panasoffee, FL

So easy to make! A dear friend gave me this recipe. I serve these every cookout and holiday. I always make extra trays... they don't last long.

16-oz. pkg. ground mild
   pork sausage
8-oz. pkg. cream cheese,
   softened

2 lbs. mushrooms, stems
   removed

Brown sausage in a skillet over medium heat; drain well. Stir in cream cheese. Spoon mixture into mushroom caps; arrange on ungreased baking sheets. Broil for 15 minutes, or until bubbly, crisp and golden. Makes 8 to 10 servings.

Remember...parties don't have to be perfect
to be a lot of fun for everyone!

Grandma's Best
COMFORT FOODS

Aunt V's Dirty Salsa

Janae Mallonee
Marlborough, MA

*My Aunt V made this salsa quite a few times. It tastes great...
it's hard to stop eating it! Serve with your favorite tortilla chips.*

16-oz. can black-eyed peas,
    drained
15-1/4 oz. can corn, drained
4-1/4 oz. can chopped black
    olives, drained
2-oz. jar diced pimentos, drained

1 red pepper, chopped
1 green pepper, chopped
1 red onion, chopped
1/2 c. olive oil
1/2 c. cider vinegar
1/2 c. sugar

In a large bowl, combine all vegetables. Drizzle with oil; toss to mix
and set aside. In a small saucepan over medium heat, bring vinegar to
a boil. Add sugar and stir until dissolved. Pour mixture over vegetables;
toss again. Cover and refrigerate overnight before serving. Makes 10 to
12 servings.

If you have a jar that's really hard to open, Grandma's trick
will get that lid off in a jiffy. Gently insert the tip of a blunt
table knife under the edge of the lid. That's usually enough to
break the vacuum, allowing the lid to twist right off.

FAMILY & FRIENDS
Get-Together

Hot Creamy Sausage Dip

Elizabeth Smithson
Mayfield, KY

An old favorite from long ago, I still use it today. Everyone likes it. Serve with snack chips and fresh veggies.

1 lb. hot or mild ground
    pork sausage
1 c. sour cream
1/2 c. mayonnaise
1/2 c. pasteurized process
    cheese dip

1/4 c. grated Parmesan cheese
2-oz. jar sliced pimentos,
    drained
5 green onions, chopped and
    divided

Brown sausage in a large skillet over medium heat; drain and crumble. Remove from heat. Add remaining ingredients, reserving a small amount of onions for garnish. Mix well and transfer to a lightly greased 2-quart casserole dish. Bake, uncovered, at 350 degrees for 20 to 25 minutes. Serve warm, garnished with reserved onions. Makes 8 to 10 servings.

Start a Family Game Night. Get out all your favorite board games and play to your heart's content. Small prizes for winners and bowls of popcorn or snack mix are a must!

Grandma's Best
COMFORT FOODS

Golden Meatballs

Carol Hickman
Kingsport, TN

These tasty meatballs make great appetizers! Transfer meatballs and sauce to a slow cooker set on low to keep warm for serving.

1 lb. lean ground beef
1 lb. ground pork sausage
1/2 c. dry bread crumbs
2 eggs, lightly beaten

1/3 c. milk
2-oz. pkg. onion soup mix
1/4 t. pepper

Combine all ingredients in a large bowl; mix until well combined. Form mixture into one to 1-1/2 inch meatballs. Arrange on a large rimmed baking sheet coated with non-stick vegetable spray. Bake at 375 degrees for 25 to 30 minutes, until browned; drain. Prepare Sauce; transfer meatballs to pan with sauce. Simmer, stirring gently, over medium-low heat until meatballs are coated with sauce. Makes about 3 to 4 dozen.

Sauce:

1/2 c. spicy mustard
1/2 c. apple jelly
1/2 c. ginger ale

1 t. Worcestershire sauce
Optional: several shakes hot
pepper sauce to taste

Combine all ingredients in a Dutch oven over medium heat. Bring to a boil, stirring constantly. Reduce heat to medium and simmer for 2 to 3 minutes, stirring often.

Dip your hands into a little cold water before shaping meatballs...the meat won't stick to your hands.

FAMILY & FRIENDS
Get-Together

Crisp Sweet Pickles

Paula Marchesi
Auburn, PA

Delicious and easy! In one week, you'll have sweet pickles...no cooking, no canning jars. You'll love making these all summer. Serve with sandwiches at picnics and parties. A pretty glass jar of these pickles makes a nice gift, too.

32-oz. jar whole kosher dill
    pickles, drained
1-1/4 c. sugar

3 T. cider vinegar
1 T. dried, minced onions
1 T. celery seed

Cut pickles into 1/2-inch slices; return slices to the jar they came in. Add remaining ingredients to jar; cover and shake until coated. Refrigerate at least one week, shaking the jar occasionally, once every day or 2. After one week, serve pickles with a slotted spoon. Makes one quart.

A big platter heaped with yummy finger foods is sure to welcome guests. Deli meats, cheese cubes, fresh or dried fruits and an assortment of pickles let guests pick and choose as they like.

Poppy Seed Sliders

Julie Harris
Mertztown, PA

These buttery little sandwiches are always a hit! This is a great dish to bring to parties, family gatherings or church functions.

12-oz. pkg. Hawaiian rolls, split
3/4 c. butter, melted
1 T. Dijon mustard
1 T. poppy seed
2 t. dried, minced onions
1 t. Worcestershire sauce

1 t. brown sugar, packed
1/2 to 3/4 lb. thinly sliced deli
  baked ham
1/2 to 3/4 lb. thinly sliced deli
  Swiss cheese

Place bottoms of rolls in a buttered 13"x9" baking pan; set aside. In a bowl, combine all ingredients except ham and cheese; mix well. Brush a light layer of butter mixture over rolls in pan. Layer with ham and cheese slices. Add tops of rolls. Brush butter mixture over rolls, covering completely and getting in between rolls. Bake, uncovered at 350 degrees for 20 minutes, or until tops are golden and cheese is melted. Let stand for 20 to 30 minutes before serving. Makes one dozen.

If you're short on table space when entertaining, an old-fashioned wooden ironing board makes a sturdy sideboard. Just adjust it to a convenient height, add a pretty table runner and set out the food...come & get it!

FAMILY & FRIENDS
Get-Together

Mini Cocktail Pizzas

Carolyn Deckard
Bedford, IN

These little treats are great for any party. I got this recipe
years ago from my favorite aunt.

1 lb. ground pork sausage
2 5-oz. jars sharp pasteurized
   process cheese spread
1/4 c. catsup

3 T. Worcestershire sauce
1/4 t. dried oregano
2 16-oz. loaves party rye bread

Brown sausage in a skillet over medium heat; drain. Add remaining
ingredients except bread; cook and stir over medium-low heat until
mixed well. Remove from heat. Spread each slice of bread with 2 to
3 teaspoons sausage mixture. Arrange on aluminum foil-lined baking
sheets. Bake at 400 degrees for 10 minutes, or until hot and bubbly.
Serves 8 to 10.

For a fast and fun party punch, combine a pint of sherbet
with a 2-liter bottle of chilled soda. Match up flavors...
strawberry sherbet with strawberry soda, lime sherbet
with lemon–lime soda. Yummy!

Grandma's Best
COMFORT FOODS

MeMaw's Trash Mix

Brenda Schenck
Titusville, FL

We all travel to my youngest daughter's for Thanksgiving, which she and my son-in-law host at their local Masonic lodge. They invite elderly people and friends who don't have family nearby...we usually have 30 to 40 people. My girls and their families always expect me to bring this, with enough to snack on before dinner, and enough to take home. Everyone enjoys munching on MeMaw's Trash Mix!

12-oz. pkg. crispy corn &
   rice cereal squares
12-oz. pkg. baked cheese
   crackers
2 c. thin pretzel sticks
2 c. deluxe mixed nuts

3/4 c. butter, melted
1/4 c. Worcestershire sauce
4 t. seasoned salt
2 t. onion powder
2 t. garlic powder

In a very large roasting pan, combine cereal, crackers, pretzels and nuts; toss to mix and set aside. Combine remaining ingredients in a bowl; mix well and drizzle over cereal mixture. Stir to mix everything together. Bake, uncovered, at 275 degrees for one hour. stirring every 15 minutes. Cool; store in an airtight container. Makes 12 to 15 servings.

When you look at your life, the greatest happinesses
are family happinesses.
–Dr. Joyce Brothers

Peachy Iced Tea

JoAnn
Gooseberry Patch

Perfect for sipping while you're sitting on Gram's front porch.

2 c. boiling water
1 family-size iced tea bag
2 c. cold water
10-oz. pkg. frozen sliced
    peaches, thawed

1 T. lemon juice
sugar to taste
ice cubes

Pour boiling water over tea bag in a pitcher. Let stand 3 to 5 minutes; discard tea bag. Add cold water; cover and refrigerate for one hour. Combine peaches and lemon juice in a blender; process until puréed. Strain peach mixture into pitcher, discarding solids. Stir well; add sugar to taste. Cover and chill. Serve over ice. Makes 4 to 6 servings.

Mother's Red Punch

Lauren Williams
Mayfield, KY

My mother always makes this punch for Christmas and for all kinds of showers. It is a family favorite.

46-oz. can pineapple juice
1 pkg. unsweetened cherry
    drink mix

1 c. sugar
32-oz. bottle ginger ale, chilled

Partially fill a ring mold with pineapple juice; freeze until solid. Combine remaining juice, drink mix and sugar; stir well and chill. At serving time, add frozen ice ring to a punch bowl; pour in juice mixture. Add ginger ale and serve. Makes 12 servings.

For some terrific summertime memories, set up an old-fashioned lemonade stand with the kids!

Grandma's Best COMFORT FOODS

Pickled Cider Eggs

Jason Keller
Carrollton, GA

This is a family favorite for snacking at get-togethers. Sometimes I'll tuck a few sprigs of fresh dill into the jar before closing.

1 doz. eggs, hard-boiled and
   peeled
1-quart wide-mouth canning
   jar and lid, sterilized
1-1/2 c. apple cider or apple juice

1/2 c. white vinegar
1 t. salt
1 t. pickling spices
6 thin slices onion
1 clove garlic, peeled

Pack eggs loosely into warm sterilized jar; set aside. Combine remaining ingredients in a saucepan over medium heat; bring to a boil. Reduce heat to medium-low and simmer for 5 minutes. Pour hot mixture over eggs in jar. If eggs aren't completely covered by liquid, add a little more cider. Immediately add lid and refrigerate; chill before serving. Eggs may be sliced in half for serving. Keep refrigerated up to one month. Makes one dozen.

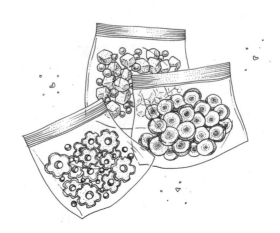

Colorful, fresh veggies are always welcome at parties and easy to prepare in advance. Cut them into bite–size slices, flowerets or cubes and tuck away in plastic zipping bags until needed...what a time–saver!

FAMILY & FRIENDS
Get-Together

Baked Cheese Fondue

Jean Still
Iola, KS

*Whenever I fix this recipe, I think of my mother, as it was one of
her favorites as it is of my sister and me. It is not a fondue as
we think of today...but it is deliciously cheesy.*

3 eggs, separated
1-1/4 c. soft day-old bread
   crumbs
1 c. milk

1/2 t. salt
1/4 t. mustard
8-oz. pkg. pasteurized process
   cheese, grated or chopped

Beat egg yolks lightly in a bowl; add remaining ingredients except egg
whites. Mix well and set aside. In a separate bowl, beat egg whites with
an electric mixer on high speed until stiff peaks form. Fold egg whites
into egg yolk mixture. Transfer mixture to a greased 2-quart casserole
dish. Bake, uncovered, at 350 degrees for 50 minutes, or until a knife
tip inserted in the center comes out clean. Cut into squares; serve warm.
Serves 6.

Keep a chilled pitcher of water in the fridge for a refreshing
thirst quencher anytime. If your family enjoys flavored water,
add a few lemon wedges, orange slices or sprigs of fresh mint.

Grandma's Best COMFORT FOODS

Gayle's Sweet Pickle Relish

Melinda Grunden
Cecil, OH

This recipe was my maternal grandmother's best friend's and is probably over 100 years old, as they have both been gone for a long time. It is the only relish that we use. I have bought cucumbers just to make this relish for our family.

6 pts. cucumbers, ground
    and drained
6 onions, diced
6 green or red peppers, diced
5 c. sugar
4 c. white vinegar

1 t. salt
1/8 t. allspice
4 drops green food coloring
1/2 t. mustard seed
10 1-pint canning jars with lids,
    sterilized

In a large stockpot, mix all ingredients except mustard seed. Bring to a boil over high heat; simmer for 15 minutes. Add mustard seed. Spoon into hot sterilized jars, leaving 1/4-inch headspace. Wipe rims; secure with lids and rings. Process in a boiling-water bath for 15 to 20 minutes; set jars on a towel to cool. Makes about 10 pints.

Fresh Chunky Salsa

Brandi Faulk
Pageland, SC

I learned this delicious recipe from my mom. Whenever Dad was working at the market, we used to have "chips & salsa" night. He'd bring home all the ingredients and we'd eat it. Yum! You can just put it all in the blender to make it easier, but that also makes the salsa more liquid.

5 to 6 ripe tomatoes, cubed
1 onion, finely chopped
fresh cilantro to taste, snipped

salt and pepper to taste
juice of 2 limes
tortilla chips

In a large bowl, combine tomatoes, onion and cilantro; mix well. Season with salt and pepper; add lime juice and mix again. Serve immediately, or for best flavor, cover and chill overnight. Serve with tortilla chips. Makes 4 servings.

FAMILY & FRIENDS
Get-Together

Mimi's Hot Dog Chili

Robyn Stroh
Summerville, WV

I got this recipe from my wonderful mother-in-law. It's delicious spooned over hot dogs. We love it because it is just the right mixture of sweet and spicy! It makes a thick chili that can be served on buns as Sloppy Joes also. If you prefer a thinner chili, just add a little water.

1 lb. ground beef
3/4 c. onion, chopped
24-oz. bottle catsup
1/4 c. brown sugar, packed

1-3/4 oz. pkg. chili
seasoning mix
1 to 3 T. curry powder, to taste

Brown beef in a skillet over medium heat until the pink is almost gone. Add onion; continue to cook until beef is no longer pink and onion is tender. Stir in catsup, brown sugar and chili seasoning. Add curry powder gradually, to desired taste. Bring to a boil over medium heat; reduce heat to medium-low. Simmer for 15 minutes, stirring occasionally. Serves 15 to 20.

A fun and simple party idea...serve up a chili dog bar!
Along with steamed hot dogs and buns, set out some tasty
chili, shredded cheese, sauerkraut, chopped onions
and your favorite condiments.

Shrimp Dip

Sjana Jackett
Manitoba, Canada

This is a favorite of all my daughters...if there is any left, they all fuss about who gets to take home the leftovers! The mixture is yummy and thick enough to use as a filling in wraps or sandwiches, so we sometimes add sour cream to make more of a dipping consistency. Serve with crackers and fresh veggies.

8-oz. pkg. cream cheese, softened
2 6-oz. cans small shrimp, drained and rinsed
4 green onions, finely chopped

4 eggs, hard-boiled, peeled and chopped
1 stalk celery, finely chopped
salt and pepper to taste

Combine all ingredients in a large bowl; mix well. Cover and chill until serving time. Makes about 2 cups.

Ranch Deviled Eggs

Vickie
Gooseberry Patch

These zesty eggs are a little different from the usual!

6 eggs, hard-boiled, peeled and halved
3 T. mayonnaise

1/2 t. Dijon mustard
1-1/2 t. ranch salad dressing mix
Garnish: paprika

Remove egg yolks to a bowl; arrange egg whites on a serving plate and set aside. Mash yolks with a fork. Add remaining ingredients except paprika; mix well. Spoon or pipe into egg whites. Sprinkle with paprika. Cover and chill at least 30 minutes. Makes one dozen.

Nestle deviled eggs in ruffled paper muffin cups
and arrange on a platter.

FAMILY & FRIENDS
Get-Together

Hot Crabmeat Dip

Christina Mamula
Aliquippa, PA

A recipe handed down from my dear aunt. She gave me her recipe box many years ago and I love to remember her by going through it and making her recipes. She was a pretty neat lady...I decided it was time to share her with others.

8-oz. pkg. cream cheese,
    softened
1 T. milk
6-1/2 oz. can crabmeat, drained
    and flaked
2 T. onion, finely chopped

1/2 t. horseradish sauce
1/4 t. salt
pepper to taste
1/2 c. toasted almonds, sliced
assorted crackers

Combine cream cheese, milk, crabmeat, onion, horseradish and salt; blend well. Season with a dash of pepper. Spoon into a lightly greased one-quart casserole dish; sprinkle with toasted almonds. Bake, uncovered, at 375 degrees for 15 minutes. Serve piping hot with crackers. Makes 6 servings.

Make your own baguette crisps to go with hot dips and spreads.
Thinly slice a French loaf and arrange slices on a baking sheet.
Sprinkle with olive oil and garlic powder, then bake at 400 degrees
for 12 to 15 minutes, until toasty and golden.

Buffalo Chicken Dip

Cyndi Little
Whitsett, NC

I first sampled this spicy dish at my son and daughter-in-law's Open House. Her mother brought it as part of the appetizers offered. It was such a hit, I had to find the recipe and begin serving it at my own get-togethers!

2 10-oz. cans chunk chicken,
   drained and flaked
3/4 c. hot pepper sauce, or
   to taste
2 8-oz. pkgs. cream cheese,
   softened

1 c. ranch salad dressing
1-1/2 c. shredded Cheddar
   cheese, divided
celery sticks, crackers and
   pita chips

Combine chicken and hot sauce in a skillet over medium heat; cook until heated through. Stir in cream cheese and ranch dressing. Cook and stir until warmed through and well blended. Mix in half of shredded cheese; transfer mixture to a lightly greased 13"x9" baking pan. Sprinkle with remaining cheese. Bake, uncovered, at 350 degrees for 30 minutes, or until hot and bubbly. Serve with celery sticks, crackers and pita chips. Serves 10 to 12.

A quick and tasty appetizer in an instant! Place a block of cream cheese on a serving plate, spoon sweet-hot pepper jelly over it and serve with crisp crackers. Works great with fruit chutney or spicy salsa too.

Cheesy Sausage Dip

Missy Abbott
Hickory, PA

This dip has been in my family for many years, with so many variations. I believe my mother told me the original recipe was done with all cheese and tomatoes. Over the years, each generation has made some changes to end with this delicious result! It's equally good made with cooked, crumbled bacon instead of sausage.

1 lb. sweet ground pork sausage, browned and drained
8-oz. pkg. cream cheese, cubed and softened
8-oz. pkg. pasteurized process cheese, cubed
24-oz. jar favorite salsa
scoop-type corn chips or bread

Combine all ingredients except chips or bread in a 2-quart slow cooker; mix well. Cover and cook on low setting for 3 to 4 hours. Before serving, stir until creamy. Serve with corn chips or bread for dipping. Makes 12 to 15 servings.

Make some crispy tortilla chips to serve with dips. Cut corn tortillas into wedges, spritz with non-stick vegetable spray and arrange on a baking sheet. Sprinkle with salt and bake at 350 degrees for 5 to 10 minutes, until crisp.

Grandma's Best
COMFORT FOODS

New England Snack Mix

Jill Ball
Highland, UT

*On cool fall nights, we love to sit by our fireplace playing
card games as a family. My family especially loves it when
I whip up this easy and yummy snack mix to munch on.*

1/2 c. brown sugar, packed
1/4 c. butter, sliced
1 T. corn syrup
1 T. molasses
1/4 t. salt

1/4 t. baking soda
1/4 t. vanilla extract
5 c. mini pretzel twists
1 c. salted peanuts

In a large microwave-safe bowl, combine brown sugar, butter, corn
syrup and molasses. Microwave on high for 45 seconds or until butter
is melted; stir. Microwave again for 20 seconds longer, or until mixture
boils. Immediately stir in salt, baking soda and vanilla. (Caution,
mixture will foam.) Stir in pretzels and peanuts. Microwave on high for
25 seconds, or until pretzels and nuts are well coated; stir. Spread into a
greased baking sheet. Cool for 15 minutes. Store in an airtight container.
Makes 12 servings.

Do you have a scrumptious party recipe that everyone
just raves about? Send guests home with a copy of the recipe,
stapled to a small plastic zipping bag filled with the snack.
They'll thank you for it!

FAMILY & FRIENDS
Get-Together

Lemon-Dill Snack Mix

Krista Marshall
Fort Wayne, IN

*My mom used to made this tasty snack mix this when I was little,
and now I make it for my family. Bet you can't eat just one bite!*

2 12-oz. pkgs. oyster crackers
1 c. canola oil
2 1-oz. pkgs. ranch salad
    dressing mix

2 t. dried dill weed
1 t. garlic powder
1/2 t. lemon pepper

Spread crackers in a large roasting pan; set aside. In a bowl, stir together
oil and seasonings. Pour over crackers and stir gently. Bake, uncovered,
at 350 degrees for 30 minutes, stirring every 10 minutes. Turn off oven,
leave pan in oven until cooled. Makes 10 servings.

Grandma always said, "Never return a dish empty." Gather up
casseroles and pie plates that have been left behind, fill them
with homemade goodies and return to their owners!

Grandma's Best
COMFORT FOODS

Heavenly Ham Sandwiches

Shawn Liebheit
Moro, IL

These little sandwiches are great for any type of get-together, but watch out...they are so yummy, they'll go fast! If you have any left over, which would be a surprise, they can be frozen and reheated in the microwave and they are just as good.

2 12-oz. pkgs. Hawaiian rolls	3/4 c. butter
1 lb. thinly sliced deli baked ham	1-1/2 T. Dijon mustard
1 lb. thinly sliced deli Swiss	1-1/2 t. Worcestershire sauce
cheese	1-1/2 t. dried, minced onions

Slice one whole package of rolls at once; repeat with second package. Place bottom halves of rolls from both packages in an ungreased 13"x9" baking pan. Layer ham and cheese over rolls; add tops of rolls and set aside. Melt butter in a small saucepan over medium heat; stir in mustard, Worcestershire sauce and onions. Drizzle mixture over rolls, evenly distributing onions. Cover with aluminum foil and refrigerate overnight. Bake, uncovered, at 350 degrees for 15 to 20 minutes; serve. Makes 2 dozen.

Put out the welcome mat and invite friends over for
a retro–style appetizer party. Serve up yummy finger foods
from Grandma's day and play favorite tunes from the 1950s or
1960s...everyone is sure to have a blast!

FAMILY & FRIENDS
Get-Together

Scrumptious Ham Balls

Amanda Bitting
Papillion, NE

My grandma always made this delicious recipe for our family and for anyone she hosted. She loved to entertain and always had yummy treats ready when you walked in the door. My mom has carried on this tradition and continues to make this recipe for family events today!

2-1/2 lbs. ground baked ham	2 eggs, beaten
1 lb. ground beef	1 c. milk
1-1/4 c. unseasoned dry	
bread crumbs	

Mix all ingredients together in a large bowl; shape into balls by tablespoonfuls. Arrange balls in a lightly greased 13"x9" baking pan. Spoon Sauce generously over balls. Bake, uncovered, at 275 degrees for 2 hours, turning balls over after one hour. Serves 10 to 12.

Sauce:

3 c. brown sugar, packed	1 c. water
1 c. vinegar	4 t. dry mustard

Mix all ingredients together, stirring until brown sugar dissolves.

Serving saucy, sticky party foods? Fill a mini slow cooker set on low with dampened, rolled-up fingertip towels. Guests will appreciate your thoughtfulness!

Grandma's Best
COMFORT FOODS

Garden Patch Radish Butter

Angie Biggin
Lyons, IL

This perfect blend of spicy, peppery radishes and creamy butter makes a delicious spread. Serve with savory crackers or toast.

1/2 c. butter, room temperature
1 T. lemon juice
2 T. fresh mint, chopped
1 T. fresh chives, chopped

1 T. fresh flat-leaf parsley,
  chopped
3 radishes, grated or diced
salt and pepper to taste

With an electric mixer on medium speed, beat butter until smooth. Add lemon juice; beat until smooth. Mix in herbs; gently fold in radishes. Season with salt and pepper; chill until serving time. Makes about one cup.

Grandmother's Chicken Salad

Cyndi Little
Whitsett, NC

My grandmother made the best chicken salad! I was so excited when she shared her recipe with me. Every time I make it, it makes me feel close to her. I serve this on toasted sandwiches, on a lettuce leaf with crackers...or eat it right from the dish!

4 to 5 boneless, skinless
  chicken breasts
1 egg, hard-boiled, peeled and
  chopped
1 to 2 stalks celery, chopped

1/3 c. favorite sweet pickle relish
1/2 to 3/4 c. mayonnaise-type
  salad dressing
salt and pepper to taste

Place chicken in a greased 13"x9" baking pan. Bake for 20 to 25 minutes, until juices run clear. Cool; shred chicken in a food processor or by hand. Place in a large bowl; add egg, celery and pickle relish. Stir to combine. Add 1/2 cup salad dressing, or more to desired consistency. Season with salt and pepper. Cover and chill until serving time. Serves 4.

FAMILY & FRIENDS
Get-Together

Pimento Cheese Spread

Tina Butler
Royse City, TX

No party or potluck down south would be the same without a yummy pimento cheese spread. This recipe only requires four ingredients. Spread it on celery or crackers, or make little finger sandwiches with the crusts cut off, the true Southern way.

1-1/2 c. shredded sharp Cheddar cheese, divided
1-1/2 c. shredded pasteurized process cheese, divided

2-oz. jar diced pimentos, drained and juice reserved
3 T. mayonnaise

Make sure all ingredients are well chilled. In a large bowl, combine half of Cheddar cheese and half of process cheese; mix well. Add remaining cheeses and mix again. Add pimentos and half of reserved pimento juice. Add mayonnaise and mix well. If too thick, add more pimento juice or a bit more mayonnaise. If it is too thin, add more cheese. Cover and chill until serving time. Makes 6 to 8 servings.

Spills are sure to happen at parties, but don't worry! Plain club soda is an instant spot remover for fresh stains. Pour a little on the spot, let set just a few seconds, then blot up any extra moisture with a clean cloth.

Grandma's Best COMFORT FOODS

Sticky Chicken Wings

Rhonda Reeder
Ellicott City, MD

Whenever we kids spent the weekend at Grandma's, we knew she would make these yummy wings for us. She didn't care if we got our fingers sticky! We loved her even more for that.

2-1/2 lbs. chicken wings,
   separated
salt and pepper to taste
1/2 c. low-sodium soy sauce

1/2 c. honey
2 T. catsup
1/2 t. garlic powder
1/2 t. ground ginger

Arrange chicken wings on an aluminum foil-lined, greased rimmed baking sheet. Season wings lightly with salt and pepper. Bake, uncovered, at 425 degrees for 15 minutes. Meanwhile, combine together remaining ingredients in a bowl; mix well. Remove wings from oven; drain pan. Brush sauce over wings; return to oven. Bake another 20 minutes, turning often, or until well glazed and chicken juices run clear when pierced. Serves 4 to 6.

A punch bowl is a festive touch that makes even the simplest beverage special. Surround it with a simple wreath of fresh flowers or even bunches of grapes.

FAMILY & FRIENDS
Get-Together

Best Fry Batter

Teresa Eller
Kansas City, KS

I have used this tried & true recipe for years. It began with the apple fritters, but now whenever I need a tasty "go-to" appetizer, this is the best!

1 egg
1/4 c. milk
1/2 c. all-purpose flour
1/2 t. baking powder

1/2 t. salt
canola oil for frying
Optional: additional salt to taste

Beat egg in a shallow bowl; stir in milk and set aside. In another bowl, sift together flour, baking powder and salt. Add flour mixture to egg mixture; stir well. In a deep skillet over medium-high heat, bring one to 2 inches canola oil to about 365 degrees. Dip selected foods into batter and coat well; carefully add to hot oil. Fry until golden on both sides and cooked through. Drain on paper towels. Season with salt, if desired. Makes enough batter for 10 to 12 servings.

Variations:

Apple slices: For apple fritters, sprinkle with powdered sugar or roll in cinnamon-sugar.

Onion slices: For onion rings, sprinkle with salt or seasoned salt.

Mushroom caps, zucchini slices: sprinkle with salt.

Chicken and fish nuggets, shrimp: Cook through; season with salt.

No deep-frying thermometer?
Drop a bread cube into the hot oil...
if it turns golden in 60 seconds,
the oil is ready.

Teriyaki Meatballs

Shelly McBeth
Topeka, KS

These delicious meatballs are quite the snack for game days, holiday parties or just because it's a chilly day!

16-oz. pkg. frozen meatballs, thawed
1/4 c. light brown sugar, packed
2 T. hoisin sauce
1 T. soy sauce
1-1/2 t. sesame oil
1 clove garlic, minced
1/8 t. ground ginger

Add meatballs to a 3-quart slow cooker; set aside. Combine remaining ingredients in a saucepan over medium heat. Cook and stir until brown sugar dissolves and sauce is well combined. Pour over meatballs; stir gently. Cover and cook on low setting for 3 to 4 hours. Makes 6 to 8 servings.

Mail out written invitations to your next get-together, no matter how informal. Your grown-up friends will love it!

FAMILY & FRIENDS
Get-Together

Grandma's Hot Sausage Balls

Beth Flack
Terre Haute, IN

A family favorite...everyone loves these for parties or even brunch.

1 lb. hot ground pork sausage
3 c. biscuit baking mix
1/4 c. whole milk

5-oz. jar sharp pasteurized
   process cheese spread

Combine all ingredients in a large bowl. Mix well; roll into bite-size balls and place on a baking sheet. Freeze for 3 hours, or until firm. When ready to serve, bake at 400 degrees for 20 minutes, or until hot and golden. Makes 3 dozen.

Raspberry Lemonade

Annette Ingram
Grand Rapids, MI

So refreshing...share with a friend.

12-oz. pkg. frozen raspberries,
   thawed
12-oz. can frozen lemonade
   concentrate, thawed

1/4 c. sugar
2-ltr. bottle seltzer water, chilled
Optional: lemon wedges

In a blender, combine raspberries, lemonade concentrate and sugar; process until smooth. If desired, strain mixture through a sieve to remove seeds, pressing through as much liquid as possible. Pour liquid into a pitcher; chill. At serving time, slowly add seltzer to raspberry liquid. Serve over ice, garnished with lemon wedges, if desired. Makes 8 servings.

Some old-fashioned things like
fresh air and sunshine
are hard to beat.
–Laura Ingalls Wilder

Mini Artichoke Tarts

Emily Martin
Ontario, Canada

My grandmother was quite the party hostess. She always made all kinds of scrumptious finger foods for guests. For us kids, she'd set up a little table in the kitchen with goodies just for us! We loved these cheesy little tarts.

2 6-1/2 oz. jars marinated
   artichoke hearts, drained and
   1/3 c. marinade reserved
1 c. onion, finely chopped
1 clove garlic, minced
5 eggs, beaten

1/4 c. dry bread crumbs
1/4 t. dried oregano
salt and pepper to taste
Optional: 1/8 t. hot pepper sauce
8-oz. pkg. finely shredded
   Cheddar cheese

Finely chop artichokes; set aside. In a small saucepan over medium heat, combine reserved marinade, onion and garlic. Cook for 5 minutes, or until softened and liquid is absorbed. In a large bowl, whisk together eggs, onion mixture, artichokes, bread crumbs, seasonings and hot sauce, if using. Fold in Cheddar cheese. Spoon mixture into very well-greased mini muffin cups, filling 2/3 full. Bake at 325 degrees for about 15 to 20 minutes, until set. Set pan on a wire rack and cool. Remove tarts from pan; serve immediately, or refrigerate until serving time. Bring to room temperature before serving. Makes 3 dozen.

For no-stress hostessing, have food prepared before
the party begins, ready to pull from the fridge or pop in
the oven as guests arrive.

FAMILY & FRIENDS
Get-Together

Warm Mushroom Spread

Zoe Bennett
Columbia, SC

An old-fashioned party spread that's sure to please.

3 T. butter
1 lb. sliced mushrooms
1/2 c. onion, chopped
1-1/2 T. all-purpose flour
1 c. sour cream

1/2 t. lemon juice
salt and pepper to taste
1/3 c. shredded Parmesan cheese
baguette slices

Melt butter in a skillet over medium heat. Add mushrooms and onion; cook until tender. Reduce heat to low; sprinkle with flour and cook for another 5 minutes. Stir in sour cream, lemon juice and seasonings. Spoon into a lightly greased one-quart casserole dish; top with Parmesan cheese. Bake at 375 degrees for 15 minutes, or until hot and bubbly. Serve warm with baguette slices. Serves 8.

Make a party tray of savory appetizer tarts...guests will love 'em. Bake frozen mini phyllo shells according to package directions, then fill with a favorite warm dip or spread. Grandma never had it so easy!

Grandma's Best
COMFORT FOODS

Olive Cheese Balls

Amy Thomason Hunt
Traphill, NC

These are a little different, and so good!

1 c. shredded Cheddar cheese
1/4 c. butter, softened
1/4 t. Worcestershire sauce
1 c. biscuit baking mix

5-oz. jar green olives with
  pimentos, drained and
  patted dry

In a large bowl, stir together cheese, butter and Worcestershire sauce. Add baking mix and mix well. Wrap one teaspoon dough around each olive; arrange on a baking sheet sprayed with non-stick vegetable spray. Bake at 400 degrees for 10 minutes, or until lightly golden. Makes about 2-1/2 dozen.

Best–Ever Cheese Spread

Vicky Dunbar
Fishers, IN

This cheese spread really is the best...simplest, too! It was originally made by my grandmother for every holiday gathering. It's so simple to make and is always the first thing requested by the family when I ask, "What can I bring?" I always make extra to send home with those few that just can't get enough of it.

4 8-oz. pkgs. cream cheese,
  room temperature
4 to 5 T. pasteurized process
  cheese dip

2 to 3 t. garlic powder
Garnish: paprika
round buttery crackers or
  celery sticks

In a large bowl, blend or beat together cream cheese and cheese dip. Stir in 2 teaspoons garlic powder; add more, if desired. (Flavor will intensify as mixture chills.) Spoon mixture into a decorative bowl, smoothing out the top; dust with paprika. Cover and chill. Serve with crackers or celery sticks. Makes about 4 cups.

FAMILY & FRIENDS
Get-Together

Apricot-Pecan Cheese Ball

Beth Kramer
Port Saint Lucie, FL

This tasty fruit-filled cheese ball was always popular on my mother-in-law's buffet table during the holidays. She told me she found the recipe in a giveaway cookbook, back in the 1980s. Serve with crackers and baguette slices.

1/2 c. dried apricots, chopped
1/4 c. rye whiskey or apple cider
2 8-oz. pkgs. shredded Cheddar cheese
8-oz. pkg. cream cheese, softened

1/2 c. toasted pecans, chopped
1/4 c. chopped dates
1/4 c. golden raisins
2/3 c. fresh parsley, chopped
Garnish: pecan halves

In a small bowl, combine apricots and whiskey or cider; let stand for one hour. In a large bowl, blend together cheeses. Stir in apricot mixture, chopped pecans, dates and raisins; blend well. Shape into a ball; wrap in plastic wrap and chill until firm. Shortly before serving time, roll ball in parsley; garnish with pecan halves and chill again until served. Makes about 5 cups.

Popcorn is always welcome at parties. Serve it simply, with butter and salt, or with a savory Parmesan ranch seasoning. Drizzle 14 cups of popped popcorn with 1/3 cup melted butter. Add 1/4 cup grated Parmesan cheese, 2 tablespoons ranch salad dressing mix, one teaspoon dried parsley and 1/4 teaspoon onion powder. Toss to mix well and serve.

$10,000 Casserole

Hope Davenport
Portland, TX

This yummy recipe came from my husband's grandma. It is great whenever you have a hungry group to feed.

8-oz. pkg. fine egg noodles, uncooked
1 c. onion, chopped
3 T. butter
2 lbs. ground beef
10-3/4 oz. can cream of chicken soup
1-1/2 c. milk
Optional: 4-oz. can sliced mushrooms, drained

1/4 c. soy sauce
1 t. Worcestershire sauce
1/2 t. salt
1/3 t. pepper
8-oz. pkg. shredded Cheddar cheese
3-oz. can chow mein noodles
Optional: 1/2 c. mixed salted nuts, chopped

Cook noodles according to package directions; drain. Meanwhile, in a large skillet over medium heat, sauté onion in butter until golden. Add beef and cook until browned; drain. Stir in soup, milk and mushrooms, if using. Add sauces and seasonings; mix well and heat through. Spread cooked noodles in a buttered 13"x9" baking pan. Cover with beef mixture; top with cheese. Bake, uncovered, at 350 degrees for 15 minutes, or until cheese bubbles. Top with chow mein noodles and nuts, if using. Return to oven for 10 minutes, until heated through. Serves 10.

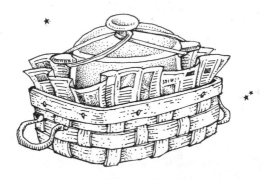

Hearty casseroles are super take-alongs for potlucks and pitch-in dinners. Keep them warm and yummy by wrapping the dish in aluminum foil and then tucking into a newspaper-lined basket.

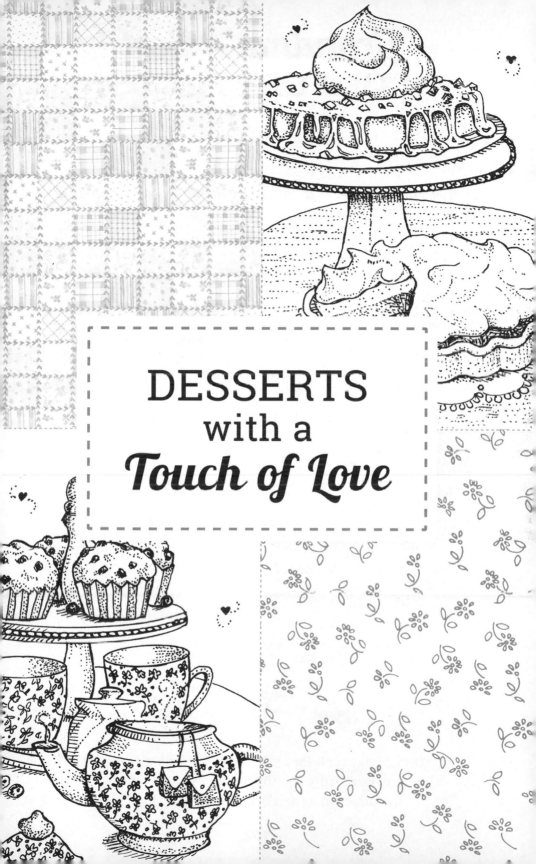

DESSERTS
with a
Touch of Love

Happy Day Cake

Carolyn Tellers
Erie, PA

This recipe has been in my family for generations, going back to at least my great-grandmother, if not further. My Grandy always made this cake for family birthdays. Her mother passed it on to her, and possibly her mother before her. This fed the crowd of relatives that always gathered for family celebrations.

2-1/2 c. cake flour, sifted
1-1/2 c. sugar
1 T. baking powder
1/2 t. salt

1 c. milk
1/2 c. shortening
2 eggs, beaten
1 t. almond extract

In a large bowl, combine all ingredients; beat well. Pour batter into a greased and floured 13"x9" baking pan, or two, 9"x9" or 9" round cake pans. Bake at 325 degrees for 20 minutes, or until a toothpick inserted in the center tests clean; do not overbake. Cool; spread with Whipped Cream Frosting and cut into squares. Makes 12 to 15 servings.

Whipped Cream Frosting:

1 c. milk
3 T. all-purpose flour
1/2 c. butter

1/2 c. shortening
1 c. sugar
1 t. almond or vanilla extract

Combine milk and flour in a small saucepan; stir until smooth. Cook over medium heat until thickened; remove from heat and cool. In a bowl, beat butter, shortening and sugar until smooth. Add milk mixture and extract; beat until smooth.

Special cakes call for special decorations! Check out the cake decorating section at a craft store for colored sprinkles in a variety of colors and shapes.

DESSERTS with a
Touch of Love

Apple Praline Crisp

Annette Ceravolo
Birmingham, AL

*My grandmother made this simple dessert in her slow cooker
all the time when I was growing up. Now I make it for
my family and it's still scrumptious.*

6 Granny Smith apples, peeled,
   cored and sliced
1 t. cinnamon
1/2 c. quick-cooking oats,
   uncooked

1/3 c. brown sugar, packed
1/4 c. all-purpose flour
1/2 c. butter, diced
1/2 c. chopped pecans
1/2 c. toffee baking bits

In a bowl, toss apples with cinnamon. Transfer to a 4-quart slow cooker
coated with non-stick vegetable spray; set aside. In another bowl,
combine oats, brown sugar, flour and butter; mix with a pastry cutter
or a fork until mixture is crumbly. Stir in pecans and toffee bits; sprinkle
over apples in slow cooker. Cover and cook on low setting for 4 to
6 hours. Makes 10 servings.

Try steel-cut oats in recipes calling for regular long-cooking oats.
Steel-cut oats are less processed for a pleasing chewy texture
you're sure to enjoy.

Grandma's Best
COMFORT FOODS

Nana's Famous Sugar Cookies

Ashley Hadley
Ontario, Canada

*My mother made these cookies for us as kids. I love them...
now my children love them too. I usually double the recipe!*

1 c. sugar
1 c. butter
3 T. milk
1 t. vanilla extract
1 egg, beaten

3 c. all-purpose flour
1-1/2 t. baking powder
Garnish: frosting, candy
    sprinkles, colored sugar

In a large bowl, combine sugar, butter, milk, vanilla and egg; mix well. Gradually add flour and baking powder; mix well. Cover and refrigerate for one hour. Roll dough into small balls, or roll out 1/4-inch thick on a floured surface and cut with cookie cutters. Arrange cookies on greased baking sheets. Bake at 400 degrees for 5 to 10 minutes, until edges are golden. Cool on wire racks; decorate as desired. Makes 2 to 3 dozen.

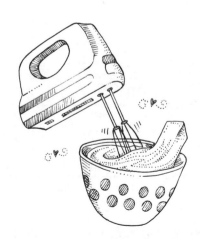

Whip up a big bowl of frosting for decorating cookies! Beat together 2/3 cup softened butter and 1/2 cup milk. Slowly beat in a 32-ounce box of powdered sugar; stir in one teaspoon vanilla extract and 1/4 teaspoon almond extract. Use immediately to frost cookies.

DESSERTS with a
Touch of Love

Festive Strawberry Cream Pies

Mary Rachel Deane
Ludlow Falls, OH

I used to make these yummy little pies with my grandmother...they never lasted long! I like to use a star-shaped cookie cutter, but you can use a circle or any shape you like. You can also use chocolate hazelnut spread instead of cream cheese.

9" refrigerated pie crust,
   unbaked
2 c. strawberries, hulled
   and diced

2 T. sugar
2 t. cornstarch
1 c. whipped cream cheese
1 egg, beaten

Cover a baking sheet with aluminum foil; spray with non-stick vegetable spray and set aside. On a floured surface, roll out pie crust. Cut out 8 circles with a large cookie cutter; set aside. In a large bowl, mix together strawberries, sugar and cornstarch. For each mini pie, place one crust circle on baking sheet. Spread generously with cream cheese, leaving the edges of dough uncovered. Spoon some of strawberry mixture over cream cheese. Top with a second crust circle; press edges closed with a fork. With a fork, pierce the center of dough several times. Bake at 350 degrees for about 25 minutes, until golden. Makes 4 servings.

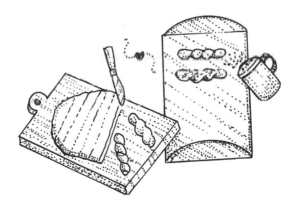

For a grandma-style treat, roll out extra pie dough,
cut into strips and sprinkle with cinnamon-sugar.
Bake at 350 degrees until crisp and golden.

Grandma's Best
COMFORT FOODS

Favorite Pecan Pie Cobbler

Teresa Verell
Roanoke, VA

This recipe has been in the Verell family for over 25 years. It is always requested for our July 4th cookout. It is easy and delicious.

1/2 c. butter, melted
1 c. self-rising flour
1-2/3 c. sugar, divided
1 c. whole milk

1/2 c. butter, softened
3 eggs, lightly beaten
1 c. dark corn syrup
1 c. chopped pecans

Pour melted butter into a 13"x9" baking pan; set aside. In a bowl, mix flour, one cup sugar and milk; spoon over butter in pan. In another bowl, mix together softened butter, remaining sugar, eggs, corn syrup and pecans; pour over crust mixture in pan. Do not stir. Bake at 350 degrees for 35 to 40 minutes, until set. Cool; cut into squares. Serves 16.

A touch of whimsy...use Grandma's vintage cow-shaped milk pitcher to top desserts with cream or chocolate sauce.

DESSERTS with a
Touch of Love

Grandma Kate's Strawberry Pie

Carol Jacobs
Anaheim, CA

Who doesn't love fresh strawberry pie? This recipe brings back
sweet memories of my grandmother and mother.

3 pts. strawberries, hulled, sliced
  and divided
3/4 c. sugar
4 t. cornstarch

9-inch pie crust, baked
  and cooled
Optional: whipped cream

In a saucepan over medium heat, combine 1/3 of strawberries with
sugar and cornstarch. Cook and stir until thickened; remove from heat
and cool. Meanwhile, fill cooked, cooled crust with remaining
strawberries. Pour cooled sauce over berries; cover and chill. Serve
topped with whipped cream, if desired. Makes 6 to 8 servings.

Granny's Lemonade Pie

Jacki Smith
Fayetteville, NC

When I was little, I would sit in Granny's kitchen and she would
let me mix this pie together. It made me feel so special to help
prepare a dessert for our family gatherings.

14-oz. can sweetened
  condensed milk
6-oz. can frozen lemonade
  concentrate, thawed

12-oz. container frozen
  whipped topping
9-inch graham cracker crust

In a bowl, stir together condensed milk and lemonade concentrate; fold
in whipped topping. Pour into pie crust and freeze. Cut into wedges;
serve with whipped topping piped on top. Serves 8.

Grammy B's Myersville Cake

Debra Myers
Randsllstown, MD

During the late 1920s and early 1930s, my grandfather was the minister at a church in Myersville, Maryland. My grandmother was an excellent partner in his ministry, using her wonderful cooking skills to feed everyone from the Bishop to those in need. Grammy made everyone feel welcome at her table. This was her favorite cake recipe, which she continued to make for family gatherings into her nineties. A bite of this sweet, moist cake instantly brings back her hugs and love.

1 c. butter
2 c. sugar
6 eggs
1/2 c. milk

11-oz. pkg. vanilla wafers,
   crushed
1 to 2 c. finely shredded coconut
1 c. chopped pecans

In a large bowl, beat butter and sugar with an electric mixer on medium speed. Add eggs, one at a time, beating well after each addition. Stir in milk; set aside. In a separate bowl, combine remaining ingredients; stir into butter mixture. Pour batter into a well-greased 13"x9" baking pan. Bake at 275 degrees for one hour and 30 minutes. Cool; cut into squares. Makes 24 servings.

Don't hide a pretty glass cake stand in the cupboard! Use it to show off several of Grandma's best dessert plates or arrange colorful seasonal fruit on top.

DESSERTS with a
Touch of Love

Grandma's Earthquake Cake

Gladys Kielar
Whitehouse, OH

Growing up, every grandmother in our neighborhood shared this recipe, so it became our grandma's cake recipe too. It's called "Earthquake Cake" because it is all mixed up. No frosting is needed for this cake. What a delicious surprise it is!

1 c. chopped pecans	8-oz. pkg. cream cheese,
1 c. shredded coconut	softened
15-1/4 oz. pkg. German	1/2 c. butter
chocolate cake mix	16-oz. pkg. powdered sugar

Spread pecans evenly in a 13"x9" baking pan coated with non-stick spray. Spread coconut over pecans; set aside. Prepare cake mix according to package directions; pour batter over coconut in pan. In a separate bowl, blend cream cheese and butter; stir in powdered sugar. Drop cream cheese mixture over batter by large spoonfuls. Bake at 350 degrees for 45 minutes. Cool; cut into squares. Makes 12 to 15 servings.

Search Grandma's recipe box for that extra–special treat you remember...and then bake some to share with the whole family. If you don't have her recipe box, maybe you'll spot a similar recipe in a ***Gooseberry Patch*** cookbook!

Grandma's Best
COMFORT FOODS

Macaroon Kiss Cookies

Charlie LaChelle Douglas
Marlin, TX

This recipe comes from my grandma's kitchen. She loved baking anything and everything! These cookies came out perfectly every time. Grandma always had the perfect touch for baking.

1/3 c. butter, softened
3-oz. pkg. cream cheese,
 softened
3/4 c. sugar
1 egg yolk
2 t. almond extract
2 t. orange juice

1-1/4 c. all-purpose flour
2 t. baking powder
1/4 t. salt
5 c. sweetened shredded coconut,
 divided
8-oz. pkg. milk chocolate drops,
 unwrapped

In a large bowl, beat butter, cream cheese and sugar until well blended. Add egg yolk, extract and orange juice; beat well and set aside. In a separate bowl, mix flour, baking powder and salt. Gradually add flour mixture to butter mixture, beating until well blended. Stir in 3 cups coconut. Cover and refrigerate for one hour, or until firm enough to handle. Shape into one-inch balls and roll in remaining coconut. Place on ungreased baking sheets. Bake at 350 degrees for 10 to 12 minutes, until lightly golden. Remove from oven; press a chocolate drop onto each cookie. Cool for one minute; carefully remove to wire racks and cool completely. Makes 4 dozen.

Kindness is always fashionable.
–Amelia Edith Barr

DESSERTS with a
Touch of Love

Margie's Creamy Fudge

Jennifer Eck
Pleasantville, PA

When my mother entered this fudge recipe at the county fair, the judges ate every piece! Margie was well known for her homemade fudge and candy.

1-1/3 c. sugar
2/3 c. evaporated milk
1/3 c. butter
1/4 t. salt
1-1/2 t. vanilla extract
1 1/2 c. semi-sweet
   chocolate chips

16 large marshmallows, or
   10-oz. jar marshmallow
   creme
3/4 c. chopped nuts

In a heavy saucepan over medium heat, combine sugar, evaporated milk, butter and salt. Bring to a full boil. Boil for 5 minutes, stirring constantly. Add remaining ingredients; beat until smooth and mixture loses its gloss. Pour fudge into a greased 8"x8" shallow baking pan; smooth surface with a spoon and refrigerate until set. Cut into squares. Makes 3 to 4 dozen.

Pure vanilla extract is a must in all kinds of baked treats! Save by purchasing a large bottle of vanilla at a club store. Ounce for ounce, it's much cheaper than buying the tiny bottles sold in the supermarket baking aisle.

Grandmother's Loaf Cake

Margaret McNeil
Germantown, TN

I didn't know my grandmother, but I know how much she loved her family by the recipes she passed down to my mother. What we call "Loaf Cake" isn't baked in a loaf pan and is actually a pound cake. The method is different from many pound cake recipes, but the result is always the same...it's good to the last crumb!

1 c. shortening	1 c. buttermilk
2 c. sugar	2 T. vanilla extract
4 eggs, beaten	1 t. baking powder
3 c. all-purpose flour	1/4 t. baking soda

In a large bowl, beat shortening and sugar with an electric mixer on medium speed for about 5 to 7 minutes, until light and fluffy. Add beaten eggs all at once; mix well. Add flour and buttermilk alternately, beginning and ending with flour, mixing after each addition until just combined. Add vanilla, baking powder and baking soda; stir until combined. Pour batter into a greased and floured Bundt® pan or tube pan. Bake at 325 degrees for 45 to 60 minutes, until a toothpick tests clean. Set pan on a wire rack for 10 minutes; turn out cake onto a plate and cool completely. Slice to serve. Makes 12 to 16 servings.

Let someone know you think they're the best. Tie a
blue ribbon around a loaf of pound cake or quick bread.
Add a tag that says, "You're a blue-ribbon friend!"

DESSERTS with a
Touch of Love

Banana Split Cake

Charlotte Smith
Huntingdon, PA

*Oh my, this is so yummy! Whenever I take this cake
to a potluck, the pan comes home empty.*

2 c. graham cracker crumbs
6 T. butter, melted
2 pasteurized eggs, beaten
2 c. powdered sugar
1/4 c. margarine, softened
3 firm bananas, sliced
Optional: 1/2 c. lemon-lime soda

20-oz. can crushed pineapple,
   well drained
8-oz. container frozen whipped
   topping, thawed
6-oz. jar maraschino cherries,
   drained and chopped
1/2 c. chopped walnuts

In a bowl, mix together cracker crumbs and butter. Press firmly into the bottom of a 13"x9" baking pan; set aside. In another bowl, beat together eggs, powdered sugar and margarine for 5 minutes, or until smooth; spread over crumb mixture. If desired, dip banana slices into soda to prevent browning; drain. Layer banana slices over powdered sugar mixture; top with pineapple. Spread whipped topping over pineapple. Garnish with cherries; sprinkle with walnuts. Cover and refrigerate for one hour before serving. Cut into squares. Makes 10 servings.

Garnish desserts with a strawberry fan...so pretty! Starting at
the tip, cut a strawberry into thin slices almost to the stem.
Carefully spread slices to form a fan.

Grandma's Best
COMFORT FOODS

Sugar Pie or Cheater Pie

Cindy Shutt
Tower City, PA

My grandmother used to make this pie for my mom when Mom was a little girl. After baking other pies, if she had any pie crust left, she would make this "cheater pie" for her. I remember my mom making this pie for me too.

9-inch pie crust, unbaked
1 T. all-purpose flour
2 slices white bread, torn
2 T. sugar

1/2 to 3/4 c. milk
1 to 2 T. butter, diced
cinnamon to taste

Place pie crust in a 9" pie plate; sprinkle with flour. Scatter bread pieces in crust; sprinkle with sugar. Pour in milk, filling about one-inch deep. Dot with butter; sprinkle with cinnamon. Bake at 350 degrees for about 35 minutes, until set and golden. Cool; cut into wedges. Makes 6 servings.

Make a fruit pie even more irresistible...brush peach or apricot syrup on top while the crust is warm, then sprinkle lightly with sugar.

DESSERTS with a
Touch of Love

Blueberry Oatmeal Cookies

Brenda Lautenschlaeger
Cadillac, MI

I had some blueberries on hand, so I just used my grandmother's oatmeal cookie recipe and added the blueberries. They are like eating a handheld blueberry crisp...yum!

1/2 c. butter
1 c. brown sugar, packed
1 egg, beaten
1 t. vanilla extract
1-1/2 c. old-fashioned oats, uncooked

1 c. all-purpose flour
1/4 t. baking powder
1/2 t. baking soda
1 t. cinnamon
1 t. nutmeg
1 c. frozen blueberries

In a large bowl, blend butter and sugar well. Stir in egg and vanilla; set aside. In a separate bowl, mix oats, flour, baking powder, baking soda and spices; add to butter mixture and mix well. Stir in frozen blueberries; don't worry if some berries break. Drop batter by teaspoonfuls onto ungreased baking sheets. Bake at 350 degrees for 12 to 14 minutes, until golden. Makes 2 dozen.

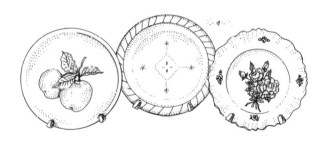

Watch for unusual plates at yard sales. They're just the thing for delivering cookies to friends & neighbors...the recipient will feel extra-special and the dish is theirs to keep.

Lemon Freeze Cake

Summer Orbin
Pleasant Hope, MO

Prepare your taste buds for a light, super-moist cake! This was one of many wonderful desserts my grandmother made for our family gatherings. My husband says, "There's just something about this cake!" It's one of his favorites.

15-1/4 oz. lemon cake mix	3/4 c. water
3.4-oz. pkg. instant lemon	3/4 c. oil
pudding mix	

In a large bowl, combine dry cake and pudding mixes; add water and oil. Beat with an electric mixer on medium speed for 3 minutes. Pour batter into a greased 13"x9" baking pan. Bake at 350 degrees for 30 minutes, or until cake tests done with a toothpick. Pierce cake all over with a fork; drizzle with Glaze. Cool to room temperature; refrigerate. Cut into squares. Makes 15 servings.

Glaze:

2 c. powdered sugar	2 T. water
1/3 c. orange juice	2 T. oil

Combine all ingredients; stir together to form a glaze consistency.

Mix up some homemade baking pan coating...works like a charm! Simply beat together 1/2 cup shortening, 1/2 cup oil and one cup flour. Store in a covered jar at room temperature.

DESSERTS with a
Touch of Love

Shoo-Fly Cupcakes

Theresa West
New Columbia, PA

These cupcakes are so moist and delicious! This recipe was given to my mother years ago by a dear friend.

16-oz. pkg. light brown
   sugar, packed
4 c. all-purpose flour
3/4 c. oil

1/2 t. salt
1 c. molasses
2-1/2 c. boiling water
1 t. baking soda

In a large bowl, mix together brown sugar, flour, oil and salt; reserve one cup for topping. In another large bowl, mix together molasses, boiling water and baking soda. Add brown sugar mixture and stir until moistened; batter will be a little lumpy. Spoon batter into 24 paper-lined muffin cups, filling 2/3 full. Sprinkle with reserved brown sugar mixture. Bake at 350 degrees for 20 minutes, or a toothpick inserted in the center tests done. Makes 2 dozen.

Host an ice cream social! Alongside pints of ice cream, set out toppings like sliced bananas, peanuts, maraschino cherries, hot fudge and whipped cream. Don't forget the sprinkles!

Connie's Comfort Bread Pudding

Connie Saunders
Hillsboro, KY

When I take a bite of this pudding, I am a little girl again and my grandmother has just given me a dessert fit for a princess! This is a recipe that I remember eating as a child. My grandmother often used her homemade biscuits for the bread cubes. I make this when I have sliced bread or hot dog buns that are a little stale, but too good to toss out. Yummy!

2 c. bread, buns or biscuits,
   torn into bite-size cubes
2 c. milk
1/2 c. sugar
3 eggs, beaten

2 T. butter, melted
1/2 t. vanilla extract
1/4 t. cinnamon
1/4 t. salt

Place bread cubes in a large bowl. Add remaining ingredients; mix well until bread is moistened. Transfer to a greased 9"x9" baking pan. Bake at 350 degrees for 30 to 40 minute, or until a knife tip inserted in the center comes out clean. Drizzle hot pudding with Glaze; cut into squares and serve. Serves 6.

Glaze:

1-1/2 c. cold water
1/2 c. sugar
3 T. all-purpose flour

2 T. butter
1 t. vanilla extract
1 t. cinnamon or nutmeg

Combine all ingredients in a saucepan. Bring to a boil over medium heat; cook and stir until thickened.

Put out the welcome mat and invite friends over for dessert... keep it simple so everyone's free to visit.

There's No Place Like Grandma's

198

DESSERTS with a
Touch of Love

Candy Cake Squares

Cheryl Nidd
Ontario, Canada

Our family has loved these squares for years! My Aunt Judi used to make us this delightful treat whenever we would go to visit. She told me the recipe had been used by my grandmother for her children when they were small. It is a well-loved favorite in our family! Look for arrowroot biscuits in the baby section...they're made for babies.

1/4 c. butter
1/4 c. sugar
2 T. baking cocoa
1 pasteurized egg, beaten
1/2 t. vanilla extract
1/4 t. salt

20 arrowroot biscuits, crushed
Optional: 3/4 c. finely chopped
    walnuts, divided
16-oz. container chocolate fudge
    frosting

Fill the bottom pan of a double boiler with water; bring to a rolling boil and remove from heat. Add butter to top of double boiler; stir until melted. Add sugar, cocoa, egg, vanilla and salt; mix well. Add crushed biscuits and 1/4 cup walnuts, if using; stir together. Press mixture into a buttered 8"x8" baking pan. Cover and refrigerate until hardened. Spread with frosting; sprinkle with remaining walnuts, if desired. Cut into squares. Makes 25 servings.

Wrapped in love! Use children's drawings as wrapping paper for gifts from the kitchen. Perfect for grandparents and doting aunts & uncles.

Mom's Granny Cake

Marsha Baker
Pioneer, OH

So moist and tasty! This one-bowl dessert was a favorite of Mom's, so we enjoyed it often as a family when I was growing up. It always stirs fond memories of Mom's love of the kitchen, every time I enjoy it now. No mixer needed.

1-1/2 c. sugar
2 c. all-purpose flour
1 t. baking soda
1 t. salt

2 eggs, beaten
20-oz. can crushed pineapple
1/4 c. brown sugar, packed
1/4 c. chopped nuts

In a large bowl, mix together sugar, flour, baking soda, salt and eggs. Add pineapple with juice and blend well. Pour batter into a greased 13"x9" baking pan. In a small bowl, combine brown sugar and nuts; sprinkle over batter. Bake at 350 degrees for 30 to 40 minutes. Pour Topping over hot cake; let stand. Serve warm or cold. Makes 12 to 15 servings.

Topping:

1 c. evaporated milk
1/2 c. butter

1/4 c. sugar
1 t. vanilla extract

In a small saucepan, combine evaporated milk, butter and sugar; bring to a boil. Stir until sugar dissolves; stir in vanilla.

A sweet addition to your baking cupboard...a heart-shaped cake pan for cakes that say "I love you."

DESSERTS with a
Touch of Love

Lemon Lush

*Shannon Reents
Poland, OH*

My grandmother made this favorite dessert whenever company was coming over...I still make this dessert today. It's scrumptious on a hot evening or a Sunday afternoon. Garnish it with additional whipped topping and a sprinkle of pecans.

1/2 c. butter, softened
1 c. all-purpose flour
1/2 c. finely chopped pecans
8-oz. pkg. cream cheese, softened

1 c. frozen whipped topping, thawed
2 3.4-oz. pkgs. instant lemon pudding mix
3 c. milk

In a bowl, mix together butter, flour and pecans. Press lightly into the bottom of a buttered 13"x9" glass baking pan. Bake at 325 degrees for 15 minutes; cool completely. In another bowl, mix together cream cheese and whipped topping; spoon half of mixture over baked layer. In a separate bowl, combine dry pudding mixes and milk; beat with an electric mixer on medium speed for 2 minutes. Spoon pudding mixture over cream cheese layer. Cover pudding layer with remaining cheese mixture. Cover and refrigerate 24 hours. Cut into squares to serve. Makes 12 servings.

Make a delicious party buffet even more inviting...arrange inverted cake pans or bowls on the table to create different levels. Cover all with a tablecloth and set platters on top.

Grandma's Best
COMFORT FOODS

Graham Cracker Delight

Pam Hooley
LaGrange, IN

When I was young, we were happy without much prosperity. I didn't realize how poor we were until I grew up! My mom would make this for a special treat for us kids, and we thought it was as good as candy, which we rarely had the opportunity to eat.

16 double graham crackers,
   crushed
1 egg, beaten
1 c. brown sugar, packed

2 T. baking cocoa
1/2 c. butter, melted
1 t. vanilla extract
Optional: 1/2 c. chopped nuts

Place crushed crackers in a bowl; set aside. In a saucepan, beat together egg, brown sugar and cocoa; stir in melted butter. Cook over medium-low heat for several minutes, stirring constantly. Remove from heat; stir in vanilla and nuts, if using. Spoon mixture over crackers; mix well. Transfer to a greased 9"x9" baking pan; press well to compact it together. Let cool; cut into bars. Makes 9 to 12 servings.

If a recipe calls for crushed crackers, place them in a plastic zipping bag and seal. Roll with a heavy rolling pin until crushed into crumbs. No mess...this works well with cookies too!

DESSERTS with a
Touch of Love

Grandma Gare's Prize Butter Tarts

Catharine Fairchild
Ontario, Canada

I never knew my Grandma Gare, but my mom talked about her all the time and always used her recipes, all of which became instant family favorites. This is one of the best!

24 frozen pastry tart shells
2/3 c. butter, softened
2 c. brown sugar, packed
1/4 c. milk

1 c. raisins
2 eggs, beaten
2 t. vanilla extract

Place tart shells on a lightly greased rimmed baking sheet; set aside. In a large bowl, blend butter and brown sugar. Add milk, blending well. Add raisins, eggs and vanilla, combine thoroughly. Spoon mixture into tart shells, filling 3/4 full. Bake at 375 degrees for 15 to 18 minutes, until golden. Cool tarts completely before removing from pan. Makes 2 dozen.

Chocolate Coconut Chews

Jennifer Bower
Winston-Salem, NC

My grandmother could always be found in the kitchen, cooking up something delicious. I have many handwritten recipes of hers, including this one. It's easy and tasty.

1/2 c. semi-sweet chocolate chips
1-1/2 c. corn flake cereal
1-1/2 c. shredded coconut

1 c. sugar
2 eggs, beaten
1 t. vanilla extract

Combine chocolate chips, corn flakes, coconut and sugar in a large bowl. Add eggs and vanilla; toss well and let stand for 5 minutes. Drop mixture by teaspoonfuls onto greased baking sheets. Bake at 350 degrees for 10 minutes; cool. Makes 3 dozen.

Fruit Cocktail Cookies

Judy Scherer
Benton, MO

*These were the cookies I requested every Christmas. My grandmother
made them and my mother did as well. Try them and you'll
find out why...they're yummy!*

1 c. shortening
1 c. brown sugar, packed
1/2 c. sugar
3 eggs, beaten
1 t. vanilla extract
30-oz. can fruit cocktail, drained
2 c. raisins

1-1/2 c. chopped nuts
4 c. all-purpose flour
1 t. baking powder
1 t. baking soda
1 t. cinnamon
1 t. ground cloves

In a large bowl, blend shortening and sugars; beat in eggs and vanilla.
Fold in fruit cocktail, raisins and nuts; set aside. In another bowl, sift
together remaining ingredients; stir into shortening mixture. Drop dough
by teaspoonfuls onto greased baking sheets. Bake at 400 degrees for
7 to 10 minutes. Makes 8 dozen.

Turn a tried & true cake recipe into yummy cupcakes!
Fill greased muffin cups 2/3 full of cake batter. Bake at
350 degrees until a toothpick tests clean, about
18 to 20 minutes. Cool and frost.

DESSERTS with a
Touch of Love

Angel Food Custard Dessert

Joan Baker
Westland, MI

This was one of Mom's favorite desserts to make...
and one of Dad's to eat! It's really yummy.

1 baked angel food cake
1-1/2 t. plain gelatin
1/2 c. cold water
4 pasteurized eggs, separated
1 c. sugar, divided

3 T. frozen concentrated
  orange juice
zest and juice of 1/2 lemon
Garnish: whipped cream

Brush off brown crumbs from sides and top of cake. Break cake into one-inch pieces; set aside in a clear trifle dish or bowl. Add gelatin to cold water and set aside for 5 minutes. In a heavy pan or the top of a double boiler, combine egg yolks, 1/2 cup sugar, orange juice, lemon zest and juice. Cook and stir over medium heat until mixture comes to a light boil. Add gelatin; immediately remove from heat. Beat with an electric mixer on low to medium speed for 5 minutes; set aside. In a separate bowl, beat egg whites and remaining sugar together with mixer on high speed until stiff peaks form; fold into egg yolk mixture. Spoon sauce over cake pieces; toss to mix well. Cover and chill. At serving time, garnish with whipped cream. Makes 6 to 8 servings.

A double boiler is a must for some old-fashioned desserts.
To be sure the water in the bottom pan doesn't boil down
too low, drop in a glass marble when you fill the pan. The
marble will rattle when it's time to add more water.

Grandma Helen's Chocolate Cake

Marie King
Independence, MO

*My grandmother always used to make this scrumptious cake
for special occasions at her house. It is incredibly decadent
and rich...an amazing cake!*

4 eggs, beaten	2 t. salt
1 c. lard or shortening	2 c. milk
3 c. sugar	2 t. vanilla extract
3-1/2 c. all-purpose flour	1 c. baking cocoa
2-1/2 t. baking soda	1 c. brewed coffee

In a bowl, beat together eggs, lard or shortening and sugar until well
blended; set aside. In a large bowl, combine flour, baking soda and
salt; stir in milk and vanilla. Add egg mixture; mix well. Stir in cocoa
and enough coffee to make a paste. Spread batter in one greased
13"x9" baking pan plus one greased 8"x8" baking pan. Bake both pans
at 350 degrees for about 30 minutes, until a toothpick inserted in the
center comes out clean. When cake has a few minutes left, make Peanut
Butter Icing. Remove cakes from oven; let cool for 5 to 10 minutes.
Pour icing over warm cake; let stand until icing is hardened and cut
into squares. Makes 36 servings.

Peanut Butter Icing:

3 c. sugar	14-oz. can sweetened
1 c. creamy peanut butter	condensed milk

Combine all ingredients in a saucepan. Cook and stir over medium heat
until thick. Immediately pour over cake.

Variation: This peanut butter icing recipe also doubles as an amazing
peanut butter fudge! Simply pour hot icing into a buttered pan. Let it
harden and cut into squares.

DESSERTS with a
Touch of Love

Apple Pan Dowdy

Denise Falls
New Berlin, WI

This recipe was passed down to me by my mother-in-law when I married into the family. Growing up on a farm, what you had in the house is what you used! Especially delicious topped with a scoop of whipped topping.

4 apples, peeled, cored and sliced	2 eggs, beaten
2-1/2 c. sugar, divided	1 c. milk
1/4 t. cinnamon	2 t. baking powder
2 c. all-purpose flour	1/2 t. salt

Spread apples in a greased 13"x9" baking pan; set aside. Mix together 1/2 cup sugar and cinnamon; sprinkle over apples. In a bowl, combine remaining sugar, flour, eggs, milk, baking powder and salt; mix well and spoon over apples. If desired, make Optional Topping: sprinkle over batter. Bake at 350 degrees for 45 minutes, until golden and apples are tender. Makes 12 to 15 servings.

Optional Topping:

3 T. butter	1/4 t. cinnamon
1/2 c. brown sugar, packed	

Combine all ingredients; mix until crumbly.

For delicious apple pies and cakes, some of the best apple varieties are Granny Smith, Gala and Jonathan.

Orange Cookies

Laurie Ritchey
Johnstown, PA

This recipe has been passed down from my grandmother...
no holiday would be complete without these cookies!

1 c. milk	4-1/2 c. all-purpose flour
1 t. vinegar	2 t. baking powder
1 c. butter, softened	1 t. baking soda
2 c. sugar	1 t. orange or vanilla extract
2 eggs, beaten	zest and juice of 1 orange

Combine milk and vinegar in a cup; set aside. Meanwhile, in a large bowl, blend together butter, sugar and eggs; set aside. In another large bowl, sift together flour, baking powder and baking soda. Add flour mixture to butter mixture alternately with milk mixture; stir well. Add extract, orange zest and juice; mix well. Cover and chill at least 4 hours. Drop dough by teaspoonfuls onto greased baking sheets. Bake at 350 degrees for 10 to 12 minutes, until lightly golden. Cool completely on wire racks. Frost cooled cookies with Orange Icing. Makes about 4 dozen.

Orange Icing:

6 c. powdered sugar	zest and juice of 2 oranges
9 T. butter, softened	1/8 t. salt

Combine all ingredients in a bowl; beat to a spreadable consistency.

The best way to cheer yourself up
is to cheer someone else up.
–Mark Twain

DESSERTS with a
Touch of Love

Grandma's Old-Fashioned Oatmeal Cookies

Wendy Jo Minotte
Duluth, MN

This recipe was Grandma's old standby. She made these cookies so often, my aunt said she believed Grandma could make them with her eyes closed. They may be old-fashioned, but are definitely a family favorite! Enjoy with a big glass of cold milk.

1 c. butter, softened
1 c. brown sugar, packed
1/2 c. sugar
2 eggs, beaten
1 t. vanilla extract
1-1/2 c. all-purpose flour

1 t. baking soda
1 t. cinnamon
1/2 t. salt
3 c. old fashioned oats, uncooked
1 c. raisins

In a large bowl, blend together butter and sugars. Add eggs and vanilla; mix thoroughly and set aside. In another bowl, whisk together flour, baking soda, cinnamon, salt and oats. Add flour mixture to butter mixture and stir well. Fold in raisins. Drop dough by tablespoonfuls onto greased baking sheets. Bake at 350 degrees for 10 to 12 minutes, until golden. Cool on wire racks. Makes 4 dozen.

Homemade ice cream sandwiches! Spread softened ice cream on one cookie and top with another cookie. Roll the edges of ice cream in candy sprinkles, wrap with plastic wrap and freeze until solid.

Chocolate Crinkle Cookies

Hollie Moots
Marysville, OH

I remember helping my mom and grandma make these cookies as a little girl. I was in charge of rolling them in the powdered sugar, so it was always a lot of messy fun! I make them every year during the holidays. The memories are as sweet as these chocolatey cookies!

4 sqs. unsweetened baking
    chocolate, melted
1/2 c. shortening
2 c. sugar
2 eggs

2 t. vanilla extract
2 c. all-purpose flour
2 t. baking powder
1/2 t. salt
1 c. powdered sugar

In a large bowl, stir together melted chocolate, shortening and sugar. Beat in eggs, one at a time, until well blended. Add vanilla. In a separate bowl, combine flour, baking powder and salt; stir into chocolate mixture. Cover and chill for several hours or overnight. Drop dough by one-inch balls into powdered sugar; roll to coat in sugar. Place cookies on greased baking sheets, 2 inches apart. Bake at 350 degrees for 10 to 12 minutes, or until just set. Cool. Makes 3 dozen.

Easily melt chocolate in the microwave. Place baking squares or chocolate chips in a microwave-safe container. Microwave on high setting for 30 to 60 seconds; stir, then microwave for another 15 seconds, or just until chocolate softens.

DESSERTS with a
Touch of Love

Grandma B's Victorian Nutmeg Cakes

Judy Phelan
Macomb, IL

This recipe is from my great-grandmother. The dough is rolled out like a sugar cookie, but thinner, and then cookie cutters are used. It has a definite nutmeg taste.

1 c. milk
1 t. vinegar
1 c. lard or shortening
2-1/2 c. sugar
1 t. baking soda

1 whole nutmeg, grated,
 or 4 t. nutmeg
3 c. all-purpose flour
Optional: candy sprinkles

Combine milk and vinegar in a cup; set aside. Meanwhile, in a large bowl, beat together lard or shortening and sugar; stir in baking soda and nutmeg. Alternately add milk mixture and 3 cups flour, mixing well after each. On a floured surface, thinly roll out dough. Cut out cookies with cookie cutters. Place on ungreased baking sheets. If desired, top with sprinkles; lightly press into dough. Bake at 400 degrees for 8 to 10 minutes, until golden. Makes 3 dozen.

You're never too old for a tea party! Make iced cookies and sugar-dusted cakes...fill dainty cups with soothing chamomile tea. A delightful way for Grandma to spend an afternoon with her granddaughters.

Pistachio Pudding Cake

Rosie DeCoito
Aiea, HI

This was my grandmother's favorite church supper cake and was loved by all her children and grandchildren. Every Sunday when we got together, we would enjoy a piece of this cake.

15-1/4 oz. pkg. yellow cake mix
3.4-oz. pkg. instant pistachio
   pudding mix
4 eggs, beaten

1 c. canola oil
1 c. lemon-lime soda
1/2 c. chopped walnuts
1/2 c. butter, melted

In a large bowl, combine dry cake and pudding mixes, eggs and oil. Beat with an electric mixer on medium speed for 2 minutes. Stir in soda by hand; fold in walnuts. Pour batter into a greased 13"x9" baking pan. Bake at 350 degrees for 45 to 60 minutes, until a toothpick inserted in the center tests clean. While cake is still hot, drizzle with melted butter; cool. Frost with Pistachio Pudding Frosting or a favorite cream cheese frosting. Cut into squares. Makes 16 servings.

Pistachio Pudding Frosting:

2.6-oz. pkg. whipped topping
   mix
1-1/2 c. ice water

3.4-oz. pkg. instant pistachio
   pudding mix

Combine both envelopes of topping mix, ice water and dry pudding mix in a bowl. Beat until fluffy.

For guaranteed crumb-free frosting, add a very thin layer of frosting to a cake and refrigerate. When the frosting is firm, frost and decorate as desired...it'll be beautiful!

DESERTS with a
Touch of Love

Cream & Cherry Pie

Georgia Muth
Penn Valley, CA

I cherish the nostalgic and comforting feeling I get whenever I look through my mom's recipe box. This recipe is among her treasured recipes, written in her perfect penmanship. She made this simple pie throughout my childhood and I continue to make it.

9-inch pic crust, unbaked
1 c. whipping cream
1/2 t. almond extract
3-oz. pkg. cream cheese,
   softened

1/2 c. powdered sugar
21-oz. can cherry pie filling

Bake pie crust according to package directions; cool. In a deep bowl, beat whipping cream with an electric mixer on high speed until soft peaks form. Fold in extract; set aside. In another bowl, blend cream cheese with powdered sugar; fold in whipped cream mixture. Spoon mixture into baked pie crust; cover and chill for several hours. At serving time, spoon pie filling over pic; cut into wedges. Makes 6 servings.

To pre-bake a pie crust, first pierce the sides and bottom thoroughly with a fork. Bake at 475 degrees until golden, 8 to 10 minutes. Allow to cool before pouring in filling.

Grandma's Best
COMFORT FOODS

Grandma's Spiced Blueberry Grunt

Doc Lorrie Poteet
Laramie, WY

This recipe was one of my mother's favorites. She received this family treasure from her own mother. I have already taught my boys how to make this family treasure. Top this with vanilla ice cream or whipped topping as soon as it is done...scrumptious!

1 c. water
1 c. sugar
1/2 t. cinnamon

4 c. blueberries
Optional: 1 t. lemon juice

Make Dough Topping; set aside. In a large saucepan over medium heat, combine water, sugar and cinnamon; stir in blueberries. If berries aren't very tart, stir in lemon juice. Bring to a light boil while stirring gently. Drop dough topping over blueberry mixture by large spoonfuls. Cover and cook over low heat for 12 to 15 minutes, until dough is done. Serve warm. Makes 4 to 6 servings.

Dough Topping:

2 c. all-purpose flour
2 t. baking powder
1/2 t. baking soda

1/2 t. salt
1/4 c. butter
1 c. buttermilk

Mix together flour, baking powder, baking soda and salt. Cut in butter with a fork or mix it with your hands. Stir in buttermilk, being careful not to overmix.

Grandma's best old-fashioned fruit desserts are always delicious with fresh whipped cream. Beat a cup of whipping cream until soft peaks form. Mix in 2 teaspoons sugar and 2 teaspoons vanilla extract...and enjoy!

DESSERTS with a
Touch of Love

Mom's Gingersnaps

Cassie Hooker
La Porte, TX

My mom always baked the best cookies! Some of my fondest childhood memories are of when my brother and I would come home from school and cookies would be baking. I can picture Mom now, pulling her canister vacuum around, and the smell of cookies baking in the oven! They sure do make your house smell good...yum!

3/4 c. shortening
1 c. brown sugar, packed
1/4 c. molasses
1 egg, beaten
2-1/4 c. all-purpose flour
2 t. baking soda

1/2 t. salt
1 t. cinnamon
1 t. ground ginger
1/2 t. ground cloves
1/2 c. sugar

In a bowl, combine shortening, brown sugar, molasses and egg. Beat until fluffy; set aside. In another bowl, sift together flour, baking soda, salt and spices. Stir in shortening mixture; mix well. Form into one-inch balls; roll in sugar. Place on greased baking sheets. Bake at 375 degrees for 8 to 10 minutes. Makes 3 dozen.

Borrow Grandma's secret for keeping cookies moist...
slip a slice of bread into the cookie jar.

Grandmother's Italian Coffee Cake

Shannon Reents
Poland, OH

My grandmother was a great Italian, and oh my, what a cook she was! I love having some of her recipes to remember her by.

5 eggs
5 T. butter, softened
1 c. sugar
1 c. milk
zest and juice of one orange
4 c. all-purpose flour
4 t. baking powder

1 t. salt
1 t. anise flavoring
1/2 c. chopped nuts, or more
   to taste
1/2 c. maraschino cherries,
   drained and diced

In a large bowl, beat eggs well. Add butter, sugar, milk, orange zest and juice; mix well and set aside. In another bowl, combine flour, baking powder, salt and flavoring; add to egg mixture and beat well. Fold in nuts and cherries; mix well. Pour batter into a greased and floured Bundt® pan or tube pan. Bake at 375 degrees for one hour. Cool cake in pan for 10 minutes; turn cake out onto a wire rack and cool. Slice and serve. Serves 10 to 12.

An edible centerpiece is so easy! Simply pile colorful fruit on a cake stand, then tuck nuts into the spaces in between. Try lemons and almonds in summer, apples and walnuts in fall.

DESSERTS with a
Touch of Love

Peanut Butter Cookies

Sherry Page
Akron, OH

My Grandma Davis made these cookies for us when we went to Kentucky every year. She measured with a green coffee cup. I put this recipe in my diary when I was 12. I added the chocolate kisses myself. Now my kids and grandkids love these cookies.

1-1/2 c. shortening
1 c. butter
2 c. creamy peanut butter
1-1/2 c. brown sugar, packed
1-1/2 c. sugar
3 eggs, beaten

3-3/4 to 4 c. all-purpose flour
1-1/2 t. baking powder
2-1/4 t. baking soda
3/4 t. salt
1 lb. milk chocolate drops,
   unwrapped

In a large bowl, blend shortening, butter, peanut butter, sugars and eggs. In another bowl, combine remaining ingredients except chocolate drops; mix well and stir into into shortening mixture. Roll dough into 1-1/4 inch balls; place on ungreased baking sheets. Flatten balls in crisscross style with a fork dipped into flour. Bake at 375 degrees for 10 to 12 minutes. Press a chocolate drop into the center of each cookie during the last 2 minutes of baking time. Carefully transfer cookies to wire racks; cool completely. Makes 9 dozen.

Looking for an alternative to peanut butter? Try sun butter, made from sunflower seeds, or soy nut butter, made from soybeans. If your child has a peanut allergy, check with his doctor first, to be on the safe side.

INDEX

INDEX

INDEX

Find Gooseberry Patch
wherever you are!

www.gooseberrypatch.com

Call us toll-free at 1·800·854·6673

U.S. to Metric Recipe Equivalents

Volume Measurements

1/4 teaspoon	1 mL
1/2 teaspoon	2 mL
1 teaspoon	5 mL
1 tablespoon = 3 teaspoons	15 mL
2 tablespoons = 1 fluid ounce	30 mL
1/4 cup	60 mL
1/3 cup	75 mL
1/2 cup = 4 fluid ounces	125 mL
1 cup = 8 fluid ounces	250 mL
2 cups = 1 pint =16 fluid ounces	500 mL
4 cups = 1 quart	1 L

Weights

1 ounce	30 g
4 ounces	120 g
8 ounces	225 g
16 ounces = 1 pound	450 g

Oven Temperatures

300° F	150° C
325° F	160° C
350° F	180° C
375° F	190° C
400° F	200° C
450° F	230° C

Baking Pan Sizes

Square

8x8x2 inches	2 L = 20x20x5 cm
9x9x2 inches	2.5 L = 23x23x5 cm

Rectangular

13x9x2 inches	3.5 L = 33x23x5 cm

Loaf

9x5x3 inches	2 L = 23x13x7 cm

Round

8x1-1/2 inches	1.2 L = 20x4 cm
9x1-1/2 inches	1.5 L = 23x4 cm